There is no way my dream would have reached reality without my partners from Magna Wave. Thank you Alane Ziemer Paulley and Pat Ziemer.

MAGNA WAVE
High Voltage Pulsed Electro-Magnetic Frequency Therapy

Thank you Rhonda Harshfield for our logo and cookbook layout.

Thank you YUM! Foundation for making a positive difference in our community.

Thank you to my Momma, Joanna Smith, for all the wonderful meals and always jumping in to do more than expected.

Thank you to all the children who submitted illustrations for the cookbook.

My Favorites Recipes

Pg _____ _____

Pg _____ _____

Pg _____ _____

Pg _____ _____

Pg _____ _____

Pg _____ _____

Pg _____ _____

Pg _____ _____

Pg _____ _____

Pg _____ _____

Pg _____ _____

Pg _____ _____

Pg _____ _____

Pg _____ _____

Pg _____ _____

Pg _____ _____

Pg _____ _____

Pg _____ _____

Pg _____ _____

Pg _____ _____

Pg _____ _____

Pg _____ _____

Pg _____ _____

Pg _____ _____

Pg _____ _____

Pg _____ _____

Pg _____ _____

Pg _____ _____

Pg _____ _____

BREAKFAST

BREAD

ROLLS

Illustration by Marilyn

BREAKFAST MAKES A DIFFERENCE

A good breakfast can help you make the most of your day. It is important for everyone but especially children.

Children who eat breakfast:
- *Perform better in school*
- *Have fewer accidents*
- *Stay healthier than children who don't eat breakfast*

Adults who eat breakfast:
- *Have more energy*
- *Concentrate better*
- *Avoid feeling tired, irritable and hungry*
- *Control their weight better*
- *Have lower risk of developing heart disease*

FRENCH TOAST

Ingredients

4 *eggs*

2 *tbsp heavy cream*

4 *slices of bread (your choice)*

Powdered sugar

Syrup

Other toppings of choice

Directions

1. *Mix eggs with heavy cream and set aside.*

2. *Place butter or oil into skillet and turn on medium to heat.*

3. *Soak slice bread one at a time in the egg mixture.*

4. *Put into skillet and cook until the toast is puffy.*

5. *Remove toast and sprinkle with a small amount of powdered sugar and top with your choice of syrup and other toppings.*

BRINN'S FRENCH TOAST

Ingredients

4 thick slices of artisan bread

1/2 cup low fat milk

1 cup Greek yogurt - plain or with fruit

2 large eggs

1 tbsp Cinnamon

1 tbsp butter

Fruit for topping

Directions

1. Slice bread into four 1 1/4 - 1 1/2" thick.

2. In a medium size bowl mix together the milk and Greek yogurt. Crack one egg at a time and whisk into the milk and yogurt mixture.

3. Add the cinnamon and whisk until well incorporated.

4. Pour the liquid mixture into a baking dish and add the slices of artisan bread. Flip each slice over once to coat each side of the bread. Place in the refrigerator for at least an hour or better yet overnight. The longer your bread soaks in the liquid mixture, the more custardy and flavorful your French Toast will taste.

5. Add 1 tbsp butter to a frying pan and preheat pan on medium-low heat, melting the butter.

6. Add the slices of bread and fry on each side in between 3-5 minutes. Check frequently to ensure the cooked side does not burn. Flip bread over once the cooked side is a golden brown.

7. Once the other side is a golden brown, remove from the pan and place on a plate. Top with fresh fruit.

(CONTINUED)

Topping Options:
warmed applesauce

your favorite jam

maple syrup

honey

a dusting of powdered sugar

Bread Suggestions:
Whole wheat cinnamon raisin bread

Cranberry walnut bread

Cinnamon swirl bread

Artisan bread can be found at Breadworks, Blue Dog Bakery, Lucky's Market, Whole Foods, Fresh Market, and Earth Fare.

Fun tip: *Once bread is sliced, use large cookie cutters to cut out fun shapes.*

Andy Treinen | WHAS 11

ANDY'S APPETIZING CREPE PANCAKES

Ingredients

1/3 *equal amount of flour*
1/3 *equal amount of milk*
1/3 *equal amount of eggs*
Pinch of salt

Directions

Mix ingredients together until mix is consistency of a milkshake. Heavily butter a pan and heat to medium. Fill pan with thin layer of mix and heat until mix firms in pan. Immediately flip the crepe and lightly brown the other side.

Crepes can be wrapped around your favorite breakfast fruit or simply served with butter and jelly, butter and syrup, or butter and powdered sugar.

Brian Goode | WAVE 3 NEWS

NO-BAKE CORNFLAKE BARS

Ingredients

- **1/2** *cup sugar*
- **1/2** *cup light corn syrup*
- **5** *tbsp cocoa powder*
- **1** *cup peanut butter*
- **5** *cups cornflakes*

Directions

Combine in a saucepan, sugar, corn syrup, and cocoa powder. Heat over medium heat until mixture reaches a boil. Add peanut butter and stir until smooth. Put cornflakes in a bowl and pour mixture over cornflakes and stir until evenly coated. Pour into a greased 9x13 pan and spread evenly. Cool and cut into squares.

Katie Bauer | WAVE 3 NEWS

POPPY SEED BREAD

Ingredients

3 cups flour
2 1/2 cups sugar
1 1/2 tsp salt
1 1/2 tsp baking powder
1 1/2 tbsp poppy seeds
3 eggs
1 1/2 cups milk
1 1/2 tsp almond extract
1 1/2 tsp vanilla
1 1/3 cups oil

Glaze:
3/4 cup sugar
1/4 cup orange juice
1/2 tsp vanilla
1/2 tsp almond extract
2 tbsp melted butter

Directions

Mix all ingredients for 2 minutes. Pour into 2 greased loaf pans. Bake at 350 for 1 hour and 15 minutes. Mix glaze ingreditents and pour over bread while still warm.

WHOLE GRAIN WHEAT ITALIAN BREAD

Ingredients

3 cups warm water

1 tsp sugar

1 tbsp yeast

4 1/2 cups whole grain wheat flour

2 1/2 cups all purpose flour

1 tbsp salt

Directions

Combine water, sugar and yeast. Let stand for 5 minutes to proof. Add 1/2 the flour and let rise for 20 minutes. Preheat oven to 500 degrees. Add remaining flour and salt. Shape into round or oval loaves and put on cookie sheets that have been dusted with cornmeal. Cover with warm towel for 45-60 minutes. Put into preheated oven and turn back temperature to 450. Bake for 10 minutes and turn temperature back to 400 and bake for 20-30 minutes.

CHEESE BISCUITS

Ingredients

- **2** cups self rising flour
- **1** tsp baking powder
- **1/2** cup Crisco
- **3/4** cup grated cheddar cheese
- **1** cup butter milk

Directions

Mix flour, cream in shortening, and add cheese last. Stir in buttermilk and drop by teaspoonfuls onto greased baking sheet and bake 12 to 15 minutes.

RAINBOW BLOSSOM
NATURAL FOOD MARKETS

OVERNIGHT OATMEAL

Ingredients

- **1/4** cup quick oats
- **1/2** cup unsweetened almond milk (or skim, soy)
- **1/4** medium banana, sliced (freeze the rest for smoothies!)
- **1** tbsp of chia seeds
- **1/2** cup chopped berries or peaches
- Stevia (or your favorite sweetner)
- Pinch cinnamon

Combine all ingredients in a jar, shake and chill overnight.

Tim Laird

CHEESE BISCUITS

Ingredients

1/3 oz sharp cheddar cheese, shredded

2 sticks (16 tbsp) butter, softened

2 cups flour

1/2 tsp cayenne pepper

1 1/2 cups Rice Krispies cereal

Garlic Salt

Directions

1. Preheat oven to 375 degrees.

2. In a large bowl, using your hands, combine the cheese, butter, flour and pepper. Then add the cereal, until combined.

3. Break off a piece of dough and roll into a 1-inch diameter ball. Place on a non-stick baking sheet and mash with the tines of a fork. Repeat with the remaining dough.

4. Bake for 15 minutes, then sprinkle with garlic salt. Enjoy immediately or freeze in an air-tight container. Makes 80 biscuits.

Note: Be sure to wash the baking sheet in between batches.

Famous Tea

MILO'S SWEET TEA BREAD

Ingredients

1/2 cup butter, softened

1 cup granulated sugar

2 large eggs

1/4 cup Milo's Sweet Tea

1/4 cup milk

1 1/2 cups all-purpose flour

1 tsp baking powder

1/2 tsp salt

2 tbsp lemon rind, divided

1/2 cup pecans, chopped (optional)

Directions

1. Beat softened butter at medium speed with an electric mixer until creamy. Gradually add granulated sugar, beating until light and fluffy. Add eggs, one at a time, beating just until blended after each addition.

2. In a small bowl, combine tea and milk, stirring well. Stir together flour, baking powder, and salt; add to butter mixture alternately with tea mixture, beating at low speed just until blended, beginning and ending with flour mixture. Stir in one tablespoon lemon rind and pecans, if desired. Spoon batter into greased and floured 8x4-inch loaf pan.

3. Bake at 350 for 50 minutes to one hour or until a wooden pick inserted in center of bread comes out clean. Let cool in pan 10 minutes. Remove bread from pan, and let cool completely on a wire rack.

APPETIZERS

SNACKS

RELISHES

Illustration by Garret

Brian Goode | WAVE 3 NEWS

SOFT PRETZELS

Ingredients

1 1/2 tsp active dry yeast

1 1/2 tsp sugar

1/2 tsp salt

1/4 cup warm water

1 1/3 cups bread flour

1 large egg

Course salt for sprinkling

Directions

Mix and dissolve yeast, sugar, and salt in warm water. Stir in flour until a ball forms. Put on a floured surface and roll into smooth ropes trying to divide evenly forming into pretzel shapes. Sprinkle with coarse salt and bake until a light golden brown at 425 for 10 minutes.

Maira Ansari | WAVE 3 NEWS

TURKEY SPINACH ROLLS

Ingredients

1 *pkg sliced turkey meat*
1 *pkg Pillsbury Crescent Rolls**
1 *pkg sour cream and chives cream cheese**
Fresh spinach leaves

Directions

1. *Roll out crescent rolls.*

2. *Spread cream cheese on crescent roll dough.*

3. *Top with fresh spinach and turkey meat.*

4. *Roll up into a roll.*

5. *Slice the roll into small circles.*

6. *Spray a baking sheet.*

7. *Place rolls on baking sheet and bake according to the instructions on crescent roll packaging.*

8. *Make sure they are light golden in color and enjoy.*

*Low-fat is fine if you are watching calories

"By the way, this is a great recipe if you have picky children. They get protein and spinach in and don't even realize it!"

PERFECT PRETZELS

Ingredients

1/2 cup warm water

1 tbsp active dry yeast

1 tsp granulated sugar

1 tbsp honey

1 tsp salt

1 1/3 cup all-purpose flour

1 egg - beaten

1-2 tbsp (approximately) of course salt

topping options: sesame seeds and poppy seeds

Directions

1. Preheat oven to 425 degrees.

2. In a medium size bowl, place 1/2 cup of the warm water. Sprinkle the yeast and granulated sugar on top of the water and let proof for 5 minutes. This mixture should have a strong yeast smell and should be foamy after 5 minutes.

3. Stir the honey and salt into the yeast mixture until the honey has dissolved. Add the flour and stir until completely incorporated. Turn the dough out onto a board or counter and knead for 5 minutes.

4. Divide the dough into two or four sections and divide among those participating in the pretzel making process.

5. Place pretzel shapes onto a cookie sheet lined with parchment paper. Brush the egg over each pretzel and top with the coarse salt or optional seeds.

6. Place on an upper middle rack of the oven and bake for 8-10 minutes, then remove from oven and place on a cooling rack.

MINI PIZZAS

Ingredients

1 *English Muffin*

1 *sandwich wrap*

1/2 *cup pizza or spaghetti sauce*

25 *slices of turkey pepperoni*

1/2 *cup of fresh spinach*

1/3 *cup of sun-dried tomatoes*

1/4 *cup black olives*

1-3 *string cheese sticks*

1/3 *cup shredded mozzarella cheese*

Options:

Pesto instead of sauce

Olive oil with salt and
   pepper instead of sauce

Fresh tomatoes

Pre-sliced mushrooms

Naan Bread

Bagels

Directions

1. *With the back of a spoon, spread the sauce on the english muffin halves or flatbread leaving about 1/8 of an inch of the sides sauce free.*

2. *If using the fresh spinach (which is a great way to get the greens into the diet), lay spinach in a single layer on top of the sauce.*

3. *Place turkey pepperoni and then the rest of the toppings on top of the muffin halves or flatbread.*

4. *If using a string cheese stick, pull apart cheese stick into strips and lay them over the top of the pizzas. Otherwise, sprinkle the shredded mozzarella cheese on top of the pizzas and place on a cookie sheet.*

5. *Place in the preheated oven for approximately 8-10 minutes. If using a toaster oven, place pizza on the toaster oven baking sheet and choose the convection setting (if available - otherwise use the bake setting). Set the temperature to 400 degrees. Bake for 8-10 minutes.*

Karen Roby | WLKY 32

BUFFALO CHICKEN DIP

Ingredients

1 *pkg (8 oz) cream cheese, softened*

1/2 *cup ranch salad dressing*

1/2 *cup hot sauce*

1/2 *cup crumbled blue cheese*

2 *oz mozzarella cheese, shredded*

1 *can (9.75 oz) can chicken in water, drained*

Directions

Preheat oven to 350 degrees. In a 9-inch pie pan add cream cheese and stir. Mix in dressing, hot sauce and cheeses. Add canned chicken and bake for 20 minutes or until mixture is hot and bubbling. Stir well before serving.

UNCLE ED'S NUTTY NIBBLINS

Ingredients

1 *regular size box of Cheerios*

1 *regular size box of Wheat Chex*

1 *regular size box of Rice Chex*

2 *boxes of pretzel sticks (very thin)*

2 *cans (13 oz) of mixed nuts*

2 *cans (13 oz) mixed nuts deluxe*

2 *cups light salad oil*

1 *tbsp garlic salt*

2 *tbsp seasoned salt*

3 *tbsp Worcestershire sauce*

Directions

Mix salts and Worcestershire sauce with salad oil. Mix well. Pour over mixed nuts and cereal in large roster pan (an electric roaster is ideal for this). Bake at 250 degrees for two hours. Stir from bottom every 15 minutes. When cool store in air tight cans.

It keeps for months.

HERB MUSTARDS 4 DIFFERENT MUSTARDS

Ingredients

8 tbsp dry mustard

8 tbsp flour

4 tbsp salt

4 tsp sugar

Minced herbs

Garlic vinegar

Directions

Either grind in a mortar, or buy herbs ground. Mix and add enough vinegar to make a smooth paste. Divide into quarters.

To each quarter, add one of the following: 1 tbsp horseradish, 1 tbsp tarragon and parsley 1 tbsp rosemary or thyme, dash of lovage, 1 tbsp sage and marjoram.

Store in jars and refrigerate.

HERB VINEGAR

Directions

Depending on the type of vinegar used, different herbs will yield appealing blends. With white vinegar, try chives, tarragon, mint, or salad burnet. With apple cider vinegar, try an herb blend or mint, basil, or garlic. For wine vinegar, use a basil and garlic mix.

Crush or bruise three handfuls of fresh herbs for each half gallon of vinegar. Put the vinegar in a pot on the stove. Heat thoroughly, but do not boil. Pour hot vinegar over herbs in a storage jar or bottle, and cover tightly. Shake often. Store for four to six weeks. Strain into smaller bottles, discarding herbs.

Cap and store until needed.

CANDIED FLOWERS

Ingredients

Sugar syrup
Tweezers
Fresh petals or herb foilage, well washed and dried
    posibilities: roses, violets, borage bloom, mint leaves
Granulated sugar

Directions

Make a sugar syrup using 1 cup sugar and 1/2 cup water. Boil the mixture until it spins a thread. Cool to room temperature. Using tweezers, dip the flowers or foliage into the syrup and shake off excess. Then dip in fine granulated sugar. Place on waxed paper until dry.

FINE HERBS

Ingredients

1/4 cup dried parsley flakes

1/4 cup leaf chervil

1/4 cup freeze-dried chives

1/4 cup leaf tarragon

Directions

Combine all ingredients. Keep in tightly closed containers.

ITALIAN HERBS

Ingredients

3 tbsp leaf oregano

3 tbsp leaf marjoram

1 tbsp leaf thyme

3 tbsp leaf savory

3 tbsp leaf basil

2 tbsp leaf rosemary, crumbled

1 tbsp leaf sage

Directions

Combine all ingredients. Keep in tightly closed containers.

PESTO

Ingredients

- **1** *cup fresh basil leaves*
- **3** *tbsp pine nuts or walnuts*
- **3** *tbsp Parmesan cheese*
- **2-3** *cloves of garlic*

Directions

Pureé in a food processor, adding enough olive oil to make a smooth paste. Store in closed containers in the refrigerator or freeze.

SWEET CROCKPOT KEILBASA

Ingredients

4 *pkgs of Hillshire Farms Polish Keilbasa, precooked*

5 *cups brown sugar*

2 *tbs salted butter*

Directions

Cut Keilbasa into 1/3 inch round slices. Add butter to bottom of crockpot and add Keilbasa. Spread out brown sugar over top, pack in as nesessary. Cover on high for 4-6 hrs, or low for 6-8 hours. Serves about 20.

PESTO SAUCE

Ingredients

2 *cups packed fresh basil leaves*

1/2 *cup olive oil*

2 *garlic cloves, minced*

1/4 *cup imported parmesan, grated*

1/4 *imported romano, grated*

1 *cup pignoli (pinenuts)*

Directions

Place basil in food processor. Turn on slowly and add olive oil. Add remaining ingredients and run until smooth consistency.

AVOCADO DIP (GUACAMOLE)

Ingredients

2 *large ripe avocados, mashed*

2 *tomatoes, finely chopped*

1 *medium onion, chopped (about 1/2 cup)*

2 *jalapeno peppers, seeded and finely chopped*

1 *clove garlic, finely chopped*

2 *tbsp cilantro, finely chopped*

1 *tbsp vegetable or olive oil*

2 *tbsp of lime juice*

1/2 *tsp salt and dash of black pepper*

Directions

Mix all ingredients in a large bowl. Cover and refrigerate at least one hour. Serve with El Milagro tortilla chips available at Lotsa Pasta.

INDONESIAN SALSA

Ingredients

- **2** *cups pineapple, diced into 1/4-inch pieces*
- **2** *cups cucumbers, peeled and seeded, diced into 1/4-inch pieces*
- **1/2** *red onion, diced into 1/4-inch pieces*
- **1** *tsp red chili pepper, minced*
- **1** *tsp garlic, minced*
- **2** *tsp lime zest, finely grated*
- **1/2** *cup lime juice*
- **2** *tbsp basil leaves, finely slivered*
- **2** *tbsp cilantro, coarsely chopped*

Directions

Combine pineapple, cucumber, and onion in a bowl. Add chili pepper, garlic, lime zest, and lime juice. Cover and refrigerate for up to two hours. Toss in basil and cilantro just before serving.

Dawne Gee | WAVE 3 NEWS

CROCK POT DIP

Ingredients

- **1** *lb of hamburger*
- **1** *regular size block of velveeta*
- **1** *can of carnation milk*
- **1** *pkg of taco seasoning*
- **1** *can of green chili's*
- **1** *large jar of salsa*

UNIVERSITY OF
KENTUCKY®
College of Agriculture

SWEET FREEZER PICKLES

Ingredients

2 *quarts cucumbers, peeled and thinly sliced*

1 *medium onions, thinly sliced*

1 *tbsp salt*

1 1/2 *cups sugar*

1/2 *cup white distilled vinegar*

Directions

Mix cucumbers, onions, and salt in a large bowl and cover with plastic wrap. Allow to sit at room temperature for two hours, then drain. Combine sugar and vinegar, stir well, and pour over cucumbers. Pack into pint freezer containers or zip-closure bags and freeze immediately. Pickles are ready to eat in three to four days.

KENT TAYLOR'S DEVILED EGGS

Ingredients

1 doz boiled eggs

1/2 cup sweet relish

3 tbsp of mayo

1/2 tsp mustard

Dash of salt

Directions

Halve eggs, mix other ingredients and sprinkle with paprika.

Seviche

PICO DE GALLO

Ingredients

6 medium tomatoes, diced

1 red onion, diced

1 jalapeno, minced

4 lemons, juiced

4 limes, juiced

10 shakes tabasco

1 bunch cilantro, chopped

1 tbsp olive oil

Kosher salt and cracked pepper to taste

Directions

Toss all ingredients in a bowl, then chill in the fridge for at least one hour.

PICO DE GALLO

Ingredients

1 *avocado, diced*

1 *cucumber, 1/2 peeled, seeded and diced*

3 *tomatoes, diced*

1/2 *onion, diced*

2 *limes, squeezed*

1 *jalapeno, seeded and diced*

1/4 *bunch cilantro, chopped*

Salt and pepper to taste

Directions

Toss all ingredients together and top cooked chicken.

Ann Curry | NBC News

POWER BALLS

Ingredients

2 cups peanut butter

1 cup maple syrup

2 cups semi sweet chocolate chips

2 tbsp wheat germ

Directions

Mix in Old Fashion oats as needed for good consistency to roll into small balls, refrigerate.

Note: Can add nuts, butterscotch chips, etc.

SOUPS

SALADS

SAUCES

Illustration by Chase

Monica Hardin | WLKY 32

MISS MONICA'S MAYO FREE TUNA SALAD

Ingredients

1 can (12 oz) solid white albacore tuna in water, drained

1/2 cup cherry tomatoes (cut in half)

1/4 red onion, minced or diced

1/4 cup chopped black olives

2 tbsp chopped fresh basil leaves

2 tbsp extra-virgin olive oil

Quinoa

1 cup quinoa (any variety - white or golden, red or black)

2 cups liquid (broth or water)

Directions

1. Combine all tuna salad mix together and set aside.

2. Bring Quinoa and liquid to a rolling boil. Cover, reduce heat to medium low and simmer until water is absorbed, 15 to 20 minutes. Set aside off the heat for 5 minutes; uncover and fluff with a fork.

3. Place your desired amount of Quinoa on a dish, Tuna on top and enjoy. It's delicious warm or cold.

Note: One cup of dried quinoa makes about 3 cups cooked.

AL'S CHILI

Ingredients

2 *lbs Chuck steak, cubed in bite size pieces*

1 *lb hot italian sausage removed from casings*

2 *large onions diced*

12 *cloves of garlic diced*

1 *tbsp cumin*

1 *tbsp paprika*

1 *tbsp pure chili powder*

1 *can (32 oz) crushed tomatoes*

1 *can (16 oz) pinto beans*

1 *can (16 oz) Northern beans*

1 *can (16 oz) dark red kidney beans*

Directions

Brown the beef and sausage in a large Dutch oven. Remove from the meat and reserve. Drain off the fat, reserving about two tbsps. Sauté the onions and garlic till translucent about 7-8min.

Add the cumin, paprika, and chili powder. Then add the tomatoes and the beef into the Dutch oven. Stir the whole pot, and simmer on the stove for about an hour and half. At that point, add the three cans of beans, simmer for another 30 minutes.

Serve with dishes of chopped scallions, sour cream and shredded cheddar cheese. A nice warm corn bread would be nice, as well.

TOMATO BLEU CHEESE SOUP

Ingredients

1 large carrot

4-5 celery stalks, small diced

1 large white onion

3 garlic cloves minced

1 cup white wine

1/2 cup sugar

1 tbsp oregano

1 tbsp red pepper

1 tbsp salt

1 bay leaf

1 large can crushed tomato

8 cups chicken stock

1 quart heavy cream

2 tbsp corn starch

2 tbsp cold water

3 cups bleu cheese crumbles

Sliced baguette

Directions

Sauté the carrots, celery and onion until translucent. Add garlic, and cook until garlic is fragrant then add the wine. Add all spices and sugar. Reduce by a third. Add tomato and chicken stock, mix well. Turn down heat and simmer for 30 minutes. Add cream. Bring back to a simmer for 10 min. Mix the corn starch and cold water then slowly add to soup. Bring back to a simmer. Turn off soup and mix in bleu cheese until it's melted in the soup. Garnish with baked or grilled crostini, crumbled bleu cheese and parsley.

VEGAN BLACK BEAN SOUP

Ingredients

1 tbsp olive oil

1 large onion, chopped

1 stalk celery, chopped

2 carrots, chopped

4 garlic cloves, chopped

2 tbsp creole seasoning

1/2 tbsp ground cumin

2 pinchs black pepper

4 cups vegetable broth (chicken for non vegans)

4 cans (15 oz) black beans, drained and rinsed

1 can (15 oz) whole kernel corn, not drained

1 can (15 oz) Rotel

Directions

Heat oil in a large pot over medium heat. Sauté onion, celery, carrots and garlic for 5 minutes then add creole, pepper, cumin and cook for a couple minutes. Stir in broth, beans and corn. Bring to a boil. Add Rotel reduce heat and simmer for 15 minutes. Ready to eat. We recommend to add some sour cream and cheese. Great with cornbread.

Lucky's Market

LENTIL STEW

Ingredients

1 tbsp coconut oil or peanut oil

1 large yellow onion, chopped

2 garlic cloves, chopped

2 leeks, chopped (use only white and light green part of the leek)

1 1/2 cups large carrots or yam, chopped

3 celery stalks

1 tsp dried thyme

2 tsp Celtic sea salt

8 cups vegetable or chicken stock* (low sodium)

1 can (32 oz) chopped tomatoes with juice

16 oz dried lentils (red lentils are most nutrient dense)

2 cups fresh spinach

Directions

Thoroughly wash and rinse your vegetables and lentils. Heat the oil in a sauté pan over medium heat and cook the onions for 4 minutes. Add the garlic and cook an additional minute. Place the onion mixture with the remaining ingredients in a crock pot and stir. Cover and cook the lentils on high heat for 4 hours or low heat for 8 hours or until lentils are tender. You can also place all of the ingredients in a large pot over low to medium heat and cover for 90 minutes or until tender.

*Make your own chicken stock by placing in a crockpot, 1-whole chicken, 1 tbs of apple cider vinegar, then fill with water until chicken is almost covered. Place lid on, put on low-medium heat for 12-24 hours. Check water levels as more may need to be added as it evaporates. Strain and use. Can be kept in refrigerator for 7-10 days.

BROCCOLI, GRAPE & PASTA SALAD

Ingredients

1 *cup pecans, chopped*

1/2 *pkg (16 oz) bow-tie pasta*

1 *lb fresh broccoli*

1 *cup mayonnaise*

1/3 *cup sugar*

1/3 *cup diced red onion*

1/3 *red wine vinegar*

1 *tsp salt*

2 *cups seedless red grapes, halved*

8 *bacon slices, cooked, crumbled*

Directions

1. *Preheat oven to 350. Bake pecans in a single layer 5 to 7 minutes or until lightly toasted, stirring halfway through.*

2. *Prepare pasta according to package directions.*

3. *Cut broccoli florets from stems, and separate into small pieces using tip of a paring knife. Peel away tough outer layer of stems and finely chop.*

4. *Whisk together mayonnaise and next four ingredients in a large bowl; add broccoli, hot cooked pasta, grapes and stir to coat. Cover and chill for three hours. Stir bacon and pecans into salad just before serving.*

Julie Shaw | Former WAVE 3 Personality

SIMPLE STEW

Ingredients

6 potatoes, diced

6 carrots, sliced

2 large onions, diced

1 large can of tomatoes, cut up

2 lbs of ground beef

Directions

Put all vegetables in a large pot and cover with water. Put the ground beef on top of the vegetables in chunks. Salt the ground beef liberally. Cover and bring to boil. When the ground beef turns color, stir into vegetables leaving the meat in firm chunks. Cover and turn heat to low. Boil gently for about two hours. The more you make the better. It refrigerates well and is better every time you heat it up.

Kevin Harned | WAVE 3 NEWS

VEGETARIAN CHILI WITH SALSA

Ingredients

Chili Ingredients:

1 tsp olive oil

6 garlic cloves, crushed

1 large onion, chopped

1 green pepper, chopped

1 red pepper, chopped

1 can (15 oz) black beans,
   drained and rinsed

1 can (8 oz) pureed tomatoes

1 lb can whole tomatoes, cut into
   quarters with juice retained

1 can green chilis

1 tbsp cumin

1 tbsp dried oregano

1/2 tsp cayenne pepper (add more to taste)

Juice of 1/2 lime

Salsa Ingredients:

2 red onions, diced

1/2 cup cilantro, chopped

4 ripe tomatoes, seeded and diced

Juice of 1/2 lime

1/2 cup fresh parsely, chopped

Directions

1. Heat the olive oil in a large pan and sauté the garlic, onion, green and red peppers.

2. Add the black beans, tomato puree, whole tomatoes, green chilis, cumin, dried oregano, cayenne pepper and lime juice.

3. Season with salt and freshly ground pepper.

4. Cover and simmer one to two hours.

5. Combine all salsa ingredients, season with salt and pepper and dollop over chili. Serves 3-5.

CHILI

Ingredients

1 *stick margarine or butter*

2 *large white onions*

2 *lbs lean ground beef*

4 *tsp chili powder*

3 *tsp salt*

2 *cans stewed tomatoes*

2 *cans red kidney beans*

1 *bottle (14 oz) catsup*

Directions

Take 4-quart sauce pan put on low heat and melt a stick of butter or margarine. While this is melting chip into the pot two (white) large onions. Put the lid on and simmer until they are well cooked and shiny. Crumble into pot two lbs of lean ground beef. Brown well, mixing it with onions. When meat is brown sprinkle over it 4 tsp chili powder and mix again. Salt well (3 tsp salt) and then just a touch of black pepper. Add two regular size cans of stewed tomatoes, including juice. Chop them into pot and bring to boil. Add two regular cans of kidney beans and bring to boil. Add a 14 oz bottle of catsup. Simmer one hour stirring regularly. Serves 6-8.

DILLED CUCUMBER SALAD

Ingredients

2 cucumbers, peeled and seeded, diagonally sliced

2 tbsp sugar

1/4 cup apple cider vinegar

2 tbsp fresh dill, chopped

Salt and black pepper to taste

Directions

Place the cucumbers in a bowl. In a small bowl, stir the sugar, salt, and vinegar together. Toss with the cucumbers. Add pepper and dill. Serve immediately or store covered in the refrigerator for up to four hours.

CUCUMBER SAUCE

Ingredients

2 cucumbers, peeled and seeded, cut into 1/2" pieces

1/2 tsp salt

3 tbsp margarine

3/4 cup lowfat milk

2 tbsp mixture of fresh parsely, chives, and dill, finely minced

Directions

Sprinkle cucumbers with salt and allow them to drain for 30 minutes over a bowl. Rinse and pat dry. Heat the margarine in a heavy skillet. Add cucumbers and sauté 3 to 4 minutes, or until lightly browned. Do not overcook. Carefully add the milk and cook until it heavily coats a spoon. Spoon over roast chicken just before serving and then sprinkle it with the herb mixture.

UK.
UNIVERSITY OF
KENTUCKY®
College of Agriculture

AUTUMN SWEET POTATOE CHILI

Ingredients

1 *can (15 oz) sweet potatoes, do not drain*

1 *tbsp chili powder*

1 *jar (16 oz) salsa*

2 *cans (15 oz) black beans, do not drain*

Water to achieve desired consistency

1/2 *cup reduced-fat sour cream (optional)*

Shredded sharp cheddar cheese to garnish (optional)

Dried or fresh chopped cilantro for garnish (optional)

Directions

1. *Combine sweet potatoes with liquid, chili powder and salsa in a large saucepan.*

2. *Bring to a boil, reduce heat to simmer, and cook until thoroughly hot, stirring as needed.*

3. *Add beans with liquid and cook another 3 minutes to blend flavors. Thin with water if needed. Heat through.*

4. *Serve with sour cream, cheese and cilantro on the side.*

JAY'S CHILI

Ingredients

1 *can (15 ounce) whole stewed tomatoes*

1 *can (28 ounce) crushed tomatoes*

1 *can (8 ounce) tomato sauce*

1 *can (15 ounce) dark red kidney beans*

1 *can (15 ounce) hot and spicy chili beans*

1 *can of root beer*

1/2 *lb Italian Sausage*

1/2 *lb ground turkey*

1 *large green pepper*

1 *large onion*

4 *tbsp chili powder*

3 *tbsp cumin*

1 *tbsp oregano*

2 *tbsp olive oil*

3 *tbsp garlic*

Directions

Sauté the Italian Sausage and turkey with the garlic and 1/4 of the onion. Sprinkle just a bit of the oregano and chili powder in the mixture. Cook until the meat is finished. Remove from heat and put mixture in a bowl. Place pot back onto heat after wiping out the grease from the meat and add olive oil, the remaining green pepper and onion. Sauté over medium heat for a few moments. Then, add tomatoes and tomato sauce, root beer, all beans and remaining spices. Cook to a simmer. Once simmering, add the meat mixture and cook for at least an hour, stirring on occasion. If the mixture is too thick for your liking, add a bit of water. Same thing goes regarding salt and chili powder.

BLEU CHEESE COLE SLAW

Ingredients

1/2 *cups bulk mayonnaise*

2 1/2 *lbs shredded cabbage mix slaw*

1 *cup white vinegar*

1 *lb bleu cheese crumbles*

1 *cup sugar*

Directions

Mix all ingredients together thoroughly in a large bowl. Once thoroughly mixed, cover and refrigerate.

MILO'S SWEET TEA VINAIGRETTE

Ingredients

1 1/2 *cups Milo's Sweet Tea*

2 *tbsp cider vinegar*

1 *tbsp fresh lemon juice*

2 *tbsp olive oil*

Pinch salt

Directions

Whisk together tea, vinegar, lemon juice, and salt. Whisk in oil in a slow, steady stream. Cover and refrigerate until ready to serve or serve immediately.

PASTA SALAD

Ingredients

2 *lb fresh cheese tortellini*

3/4 *lb mozzarella, cubed*

2/3 *lb snow peas, blanched*

8 *oz red pepper, chopped and drained*

4-6 *green onion, chopped*

Dressing:

1/4 *cup white wine vinegar*

1/4 *cup lemon juice*

1 *tbsp Dijon mustard*

3 *garlic cloves, finely minced*

1 *cup olive oil*

Chopped fresh parsley to taste

Fresh pepper to taste

Directions

Whisk dressing ingredients together; boil pasta, drain and rinse with cold water. Toss all together in a large bowl, chill, and serve. May be stored for three to five days.

HARRY'S DRESSING

Ingredients

1 *cup cottage cheese*

1 *sour cream*

1 *cup salad oil*

1/3 *cup red wine vinegar*

3/4 *cup mayonnaise*

2 *tbsp yellow onions, finely chopped*

1/3 *tsp salt*

1/3 *white pepper*

1 *tbsp dried chives*

1/8 *dried parsley flakes*

Directions

1. *Mix oil, vinegar, onions, herbs and spices together in a large bowl.*

2. *Add the mayonnaise to the mixture and whip until blended.*

3. *Add cottage cheese and sour cream to the mixture and whip until blended refrigerate.*

Harry's dressing was the Bristol House Dressing from the day we opened to the present. It still is our most popular dressing having helped the Bristol win Best of Louisville "Best House Salad".

This recipe is intended for personal use only.

Remember Bristol Catering for your party plans. Catering to you… in your home, office or rental venue. Visit our website bristolcatering.com or the Bristol website at bristolbarandgrille.com

ALMOND CHICKEN SALAD

Ingredients

1 *can (8 oz) pineapple tidbits, packed with natural juices, drained*

1 *can (15 oz) Mandarin Oranges, drained (or 1 cup grape halves)*

2 *cups cooked chicken or turkey, diced (or 10 oz can white chicken, drained)*

1/4 *cup light mayo or light salad dressing*

1/4 *cup non-fat plain yogurt*

1/4 *cup slivered almonds*

Directions

Mix fruit and chicken or turkey together in a medium bowl. Mix mayo and yogurt and fold into the fruit/chicken, gently stir in almonds. Serves 4.

Chuck Casteel | Former WAVE Radio and Television Personality

CHUCK CASTEEL'S GOULASH

Ingredients

1-1 1/2 *stew beef*

4 *cups egg noodles*

1 *can cream of mushroom soup*

1 *medium onion, diced*

Directions

Brown stew beef and cook in pressure cooker for 35 minutes. Prepare egg noodles. Sauté onion in butter until tender. Combine onion, beef, noodles and mushroom soup in a pan. Salt and pepper to taste and simmer for 15 minutes.

JACK GALLO'S GREAT GOULASH

Ingredients

2 1/2 *lbs round steak cut in ½ cubes*

1 *cup chopped onion*

1 *glove of garlic*

1/4 *cup of all purpose flour*

1 1/2 *tbsp paprika*

1 1/2 *tsp salt*

1/4 *tsp pepper*

1/4 *tsp thyme*

2 *bay leaves*

1 *No. 2-1/2 can tomatoes*

1 *cup dairy sour cream*

Directions

Brown meat, half at a time in ¼ cup hot fat. Reduce heat, add onion and garlic. Cook onion until tender but not brown. Blend flour & seasonings and add tomatoes.

Cover; simmer, stirring occasionally, until meat is tender, about one hour. Stir often toward end of cooking, stir in sour cream. Serve at once over hot noodles. Serves 8.

Dawne Gee | WAVE 3 NEWS

WHITE CHILI

Ingredients

2 *cans of northern beans*

1 *can chicken broth*

1 *can Cream of Mushroom soup*

1 *small can of chopped chilis*

Garlic to taste

1/2 *onion, chopped*

4 *chicken breasts, seasoned, grilled or baked (for ease get a bag of already grilled or cooked chicken)*

1 *tbsp cilantro*

1 *tsp cumin*

1/4 *tsp cayenne pepper*

Directions

Sauté onions and garlic and add to all remaining ingredients in a pot. Let simmer to taste. Add sour cream and shredded cheese on the side.

ASIAN SLAW

Ingredients

2 *pkgs pre-made slaw (NO RED CABBAGE)*

4 *green onions*

1 *small packet slivered almonds*

1 *tsp salt*

1/2 *tsp pepper*

2 *tbsp vinegar*

1/4 *cup oil*

1 *pkg Chicken Ramen Noodles*

Directions

1. *Put two packages of cole slaw in large mixing bowl. Cut green onion stems into fine pieces and mix with slaw. Slightly toasted almonds. Add to slaw. Mix well.*

2. *Break up and crush uncooked Ramen noodles in package (do not use the Ramen flavor pack yet). Put noodles in slaw and toss together. You may want to put just a few drops of oil in to help all the flavors begin to melt together. Set aside.*

3. *In separate bowl, mix vinegar and salt. Then add pepper and oil. Now add Ramen chicken flavor pack. Mix ingredients together well and pour over slaw. Toss together and enjoy!!!*

SIMPLE, PERFECT CHILI

Ingredients

2 *lbs ground beef*

2 *cloves garlic, chopped*

1 *can (8 oz) tomato sauce*

2 *tbsp chili powder*

1 *tsp ground cumin*

1 *tsp ground oregano*

1 *tsp salt*

1/4 *tsp cayenne pepper*

1/4 *cup masa harina (corn flour, found in the Mexican food section of many supermarkets)*

1 *can (15 oz) kidney beans, drained and rinsed*

1 *can (15 oz) pinto beans, drained and rinsed*

Shredded Cheddar, for serving

Chopped onions, for serving

Tortilla chips, for serving

Lime wedges, for serving

Directions

Place the ground beef in a large pot and throw in the garlic. Cook over medium heat until browned. Drain off the excess fat, and then pour in the tomato sauce, chili powder, cumin, oregano, salt and cayenne. Stir together well, cover, and then reduce the heat to low. Simmer for 1 hour, stirring occasionally. If the mixture becomes overly dry, add 1/2 cup water at a time as needed.

After an hour, place the masa harina in a small bowl. Add 1/2 cup water and stir together with a fork. Dump the masa mixture into the chili. Stir together well, and then taste and adjust the seasonings. Add more masa paste and/or water to get the chili to your preferred consistency, or to add more corn flavor. Add the beans and simmer for 10 minutes. Serve with shredded Cheddar, chopped onions, tortilla chips and lime wedges.

SESAME KALE SALAD

Ingredients

2 tbsp olive oil

1 tbsp toasted sesame oil

1/4 cup rice wine vinegar

1 tsp unrefined sugar

1/2 tsp sea salt

1/2 tsp ground pepper

8 oz curly kale, de-stemmed and chopped

2 tbsp toasted sesame seeds

Directions

In a large bowl whisk the first six ingredients together until thoroughly combined and sugar has dissolved. Add kale and mix to coat. Sprinkle with toasted sesame seeds and mix again. Allow to sit for 30 minutes or longer for best flavor.

BROCCOLI SALAD SUPREME

Ingredients

- **4** cups raw broccoli, chopped
- **1** cup celery, chopped
- **1/4** cup green onion, chopped
- **1/2** lb bacon, fried crisp and crumbled
- **2/3** cup slivered almonds, toasted
- **1** cup seedless green grapes
- **1** cup seedless red grapes
- **1/3** cup sugar
- **1** cup mayonnaise
- **1** tbsp vinegar

Directions

Toss together the vegetables, bacon, almonds, and grapes. Mix sugar, mayonnaise, and vinegar to make a dressing. Pour dressing over the mixture and stir gently to allow the dressing to evenly coat the ingredients. Refrigerate the mixture overnight before serving or as time allows.

Read more at: http://www.foodnetwork.com/recipes/ree-drummond/simple-perfect-chili-recipe.html?oc=linkback

BROCCOLI STIR-FRY

Ingredients

2 tbsp sesame seed oil

1/2 cup walnuts, broken or chopped coarsely

1/4 cup green onions, chopped with tops

4 cups broccoli florets

1/4 cup red pepper strips

2 tbsp lite soy sauce

Directions

Heat oil until hot in a large, heavy skillet. Add walnuts and onions and stir-fry for one minute, tossing constantly. Add broccoli and continue to toss for three to four minutes. Add red pepper strips and soy sauce and continue to cook one minute longer. Serve immediately.

Read more at: http://www.foodnetwork.com/recipes/ree-drummond/simple-perfect-chili-recipe.html?oc=linkback

SWEET & SOUR BROCCOLI

Ingredients

Vegetable Salad:

2 cups broccoli florets

2 cups cauliflower florets

1/2 lb fresh mushrooms, cut in half

1 bunch green onions, chopped

Dressing:

1/2 cup sugar

1/2 cup vegetable oil

2 tbsp wine vinegar

1 tsp celery seed

3/4 tsp salt

1 tsp paprika

2 tbsp green onion, minced

Dash garlic powder

Directions

Combine vegetables for salad. Combine dressing ingredients and shake vigorously in a tightly sealed container. Pour dressing over vegetables. Chill at least three hours before serving.

Kent Spencer | WHAS 11

CROCKPOT CHICKEN TACO CHILI

Ingredients

1 *cup onion, chopped*

1 *can (16 oz) black beans*

1 *can (16 oz) kidney beans*

1 *can (8 oz) tomato sauce (used a 16 oz can)*

10 *oz package frozen corn kernels (used 2 small cans of corn kernels)*

2 *cans (14 1/2 oz) diced tomatoes with chilies*
   (used a 28 oz can of diced tomatoes)

1 *packet taco seasoning*

1 *tbsp cumin*

1 *tbsp chili powder*

3 *chicken breasts, boneless and skinless*

chili peppers, chopped (optional)

chopped fresh cilantro

Directions

Combine beans, onion, chili peppers, corn, tomato sauce, cumin, chili powder and taco seasoning in a slow cooker. Place chicken on top and cover. Cook on low for 10 hours or on high for six hours. Half hour before serving, remove chicken and shred. Return chicken to slow cooker and stir in. Top with fresh cilantro. Also try it with low fat cheese and sour cream.

VEGETABLES

Illustration by Peyton

CANDIED YAMS WITH APPLES

Ingredients

3 lbs yams peeled and cut into 1" pieces

1 lb apples peeled and cut into 1/2" pieces

4 tbsp unsalted butter melted

1/4 cup honey

1 tsp salt

1/2 tsp nutmeg (or to taste)

2 tbsp cinnamon (or more to taste)

Directions

Preheat oven to 350 degrees. Toss all ingredients in a large bowl, combine well. Transfer to a baking dish and bake stirring occasionally until yams are tender, about one hour. Increase oven to 500 degrees and bake until liquid evaporates and yams brown, about 10 to 15 minutes.

JACK FRY'S

COLLARD GREENS

Ingredients

2 *bunches of collard greens, de-stemmed and washed*

1/2 *lb smoked bacon, diced*

1 *cup brown sugar*

1 *cup bourbon*

1 *onion, diced*

1 *tsp crushed red pepper*

1 *quart chicken stock or broth*

1 *red bell pepper, diced*

Directions

Remove stem from collards, and dice or tear into about 1x1 inch squares. Wash thoroughly as there is a lot of dirt and grit in between the leaves. Render bacon in medium stock pot until crispy. Add onion, red pepper, brown sugar and crushed red pepper to the bacon and let caramelize in bacon fat. Once onions are translucent, add bourbon and let reduce by half. Add cleaned collard greens and chicken stock. Let this simmer, covered, for about 30 minutes or until the greens are tender and sweet.

GARLIC & CHEESE GRITS

Ingredients

9 cups water

1 1/2 tsp salt

1 tbsp garlic powder

2 1/4 cups grits

4 whole eggs

1 cup liquid butter

1 cup 2% milk

10 oz shredded cheddar

Directions

1. Boil water, add salt and garlic powder.

2. Add grits and reduce heat to simmer.

3. Cook for 10 minutes, stirring often, then turn off heat.

4. Mix eggs, milk and butter. Add mixture to grits and mix together. Add 1/2 of the cheese to grits.

5. Lightly coat the 9x13 pan with bacon grease. Pour into pan and top with remaining cheddar cheese. Bake for 35-40 minutes (some ovens may require more or less baking time).

UK Plate it Up & Extension Service's

TRICKS OF THE TRADE

1 Add blended vegetables such as spinach to spaghetti sauce, soups and casserole. Children generally do not know they are included and they get the health benefit of the vegetable.

2 Prepare vegetables in a way in which they are tender but crisp. Children tend to dislike mushy vegetables and many prefer raw vegetables for this reason.

3 Make food fun. Let children create funny faces or animals with cut up vegetables.

4 Let children help prepare vegetable recipes, they generally enjoy what they have made.

Keith Kaiser | WDRB

GRANDMA KAISER'S CINNAMON CORN

Ingredients

4 *cans (12 ounce) corn, drained*

1 *cup butter*

1 *cup sugar*

2 *tbs flour*

1 *cup evaporated milk*

4 *eggs, beaten*

1 1/2 *tsp baking powder*

Topping:

2 *tbsp butter, melted*

1/2 *cup sugar*

1 *tsp cinnamon*

Directions

In a large pan melt butter and sugar on medium heat. Once melted add the flour, mix well. Slowly stir in the evaporated milk. Add the egg and baking powder. Fold in the corn. Pour this mixture into a buttered 9x13 baking dish. Bake for 40 minutes in a 350 degree oven.

Take out of oven and pour the melted topping butter on top making sure to cover the entire dish. Mix the sugar and cinnamon and sprinkle over the top.

BACON FRIED RICE

Ingredients

2 cups of rice (which yields about six cups rice)

5 eggs

6 green onions, sliced

1 pkg bacon

1 pkg(16 oz) frozen peas/carrots

Soy sauce

Pepper

Directions

In a wok or frying pan over medium-high heat, cook bacon that is sliced in small pieces until semi-crisp. Drain most of the oil.

Then, cook scrambled eggs. Add sliced green onions. Add cooked rice and frozen peas and carrots. Add soy sauce and pepper to taste. If you need more oil, you can add vegetable oil while cooking.

Note: If you don't want to use bacon, you can substitute ham, chicken, pork. etc. And, you can mix brown and white rice together to make it healthier.

ITALIAN FRIED GREEN BEANS

Ingredients

1 lb Italian green beans, cooked

1/4 tsp cayenne pepper

1 cup buttermilk

1 cup cornmeal

Romano cheese

Italian flat leaf parsley

Salt

Directions

Toss 1 lb cooked raw Italian green beans with salt. Add cayenne pepper and 1 cup buttermilk, soak for 20 minutes. Season 1 cup of cormeal with salt and cayenne. Dredge the beans in the cornmeal, deep-fry in 370 degree vegetable oil until golden brown, 3 minutes. Place on platter and shake with grated Romano cheese and garnish with Italian flat leaf parsley.

CABBAGE PECAN TOSS

Ingredients

1 cup cabbage, coarsely shredded

1/2 cup carrot, shredded

1/4 cup onion, sliced

2 tbsp water

1 tbsp margarine or butter, melted

1 tsp Dijon-style mustard

1/4 cup chopped pecans, toasted

Directions

In a large pan combine cabbage, carrot, onion, and 2 tbsp water. Cook, covered, over medium heat for 5 to 7 minutes, then drain. Add margarine or butter, mustard, and pecans. Stir together and serve hot. Serves 8.

SCALLOPED CABBAGE

Ingredients

4 cups cabbage, shredded

1 cup American, Parmesan, or Swiss cheese, grated

1 cup canned tomatoes

2 tbsp water

Directions

Cook cabbage in small amount of boiling water for 10 minutes, then drain. Grease large baking dish, using vegetable cooking spray or margarine. Place cabbage and tomatoes (season if desired) in layers, sprinkling each layer with cheese and ending with a cheese layer. Bake at 350 for 30 minutes. Serves 8.

Katherine Kington | WAVE 3 NEWS

SPRING PEAS WITH MINT

Ingredients

1 *tbsp butter*

1 *cup sliced green onions*

2 *garlic cloves, minced*

4 *cups shelled green peas (about 3 1/2 pounds unshelled)*

1 *cup water*

1 *cup fat-free, less-sodium chicken broth*

1 *tbsp honey*

1/2 *tsp salt*

1/4 *cup chopped fresh mint*

Directions

Melt butter in a medium saucepan over medium-high heat. Add onions and garlic; sauté 1 minute. Add peas (if frozen don't need to thaw), water, broth, honey, and salt; bring to a boil. Reduce heat, and simmer 12 minutes or until peas are tender. Remove from heat; stir in mint. Serve with a slotted spoon.

"My family and I have laughed and cried at that table longer than just the sum of our meals. We became a family at that table. The four of us are pretty tough, and I would suspect it's the result of the talks from that table. In high school at Ballard I often looked forward to dinner when I could be away from everything and sort things out with my parents. Family dinners sometimes force you to talk, or sometimes you can't get there fast enough to talk, but I think when you share a meal together every night and take turns sharing your day it's therapeutic. It teaches you to listen, to understand, to offer advice and to know when advice isn't wanted. Most importantly, you get to enjoy yummy food! That's the real reason we're all there. Sometimes it's going to be a frozen vegetable mix sautéed and cooking a quick chicken breast or something fast. Family dinners don't have to be all Martha Stewart, just filled with love."

ROASTED & PUREED GARLIC CAULIFLOWER

Ingredients

2 *heads cauliflower, core removed, cut into florets*

1 *tbsp olive oil*

2 *cups 1% milk*

1 *tsp salt*

1 *tbsp unsalted butter*

1/2 *bunch chives, minced for garnish*

Directions

Preheat oven to 350 degrees. On a sheet tray, spread 1/4 of the florets with the oil, season with salt and bake until caramelized, about 25 minutes. Meanwhile, combine remaining cauliflower, milk and half a teaspoon of salt in a medium saucepan over medium heat. Bring mixture to a simmer, cover, and cook until cauliflower is tender, about 20 to 25 minutes. Strain cauliflower from milk mixture, reserving broth. Transfer cauliflower to a blender. Add remaining 1/2 teaspoon of salt and butter to the blender. Add half of the reserved milk liquid. Secure top on blender and puree mixture until smooth. If mixture is too thick, thin by adding some of the remaining liquid. Season, to taste. Serve in a large serving bowl topped with caramelized florets and chives. Can add Parmesan cheese on top to make it cheesy.

MAIN DISHES

PASTA

Illustration by Peyton

BOURBON HONEY CHICKEN, POTATOES & VEGETABLES

Ingredients

2 oz Montreal Seasoning

1 oz Old Bay Seasoningz

1 tbsp fresh garlic

2 tbsp honey

1 lemon (juice and zest)

Salt & cracked black pepper to taste

Sauce:

1 oz Kentucky Bourbon

2 tbsp Whole grain Mustard

4 oz Lemon Herb Marinade

2 tbsp Honey

Potatoes:

8 medium size Red Potatoes small diced

1 tsp Smoked Paprika

3 tbsp Coarse Ground Steak Seasoning

1 tbsp fresh garlic

Pinch of chopped Italian Parsley

1 oz canola

Vegetables:

1 yellow squash, Julienne or cut into matchsticks
    only using the colorful outer flesh

1 zucchini, Julienne or cut into matchsticks only using the colorful outer flesh

1 red peppers julienne

1/4 red onion, thinly sliced

2 oz fennel, thinly sliced

Pinch of fresh oregano and parsley

Salt and cracked black pepper

3 oz olive oil

(CONTINUED)

Directions

Chicken:

Mix dry ingredients together to create your rub and "sprinkle". Half the mixture will be used to coat the chicken along with the garlic, lemon juice/zest and honey in a large bowl. Let rest in marinade for 20 minutes the place on a flat surface to "sprinkle" the remaining seasoning mixture evenly on both sides. Put in a baking pan covered with foil. Place in preheated 350 degree oven for 35 minutes. Remove from oven, uncover and place back in oven for another 15 minutes to get that crisp on the skin.

Potatoes:

Mix all ingredients in a large bowl then add potatoes to the mixture coating potatoes completely. Put in a baking pan covered with foil. Place in preheated 350 oven for 35 minutes, remove from oven, uncover and place back in the oven for another 15 minutes to get that crisp on the skin.

Combine ingredients for sauce in a bowl, mix well and reserve for plate up.

After removing chicken and potatoes from the oven to rest, drizzle a bit of your sauce over it.

Vegetables:

In a saucepan start with olive oil allowing it to reach almost "smoke" point, add zucchini, squash first and get those going to ensure good caramelization on your vegetables. Next go with the fennel, peppers, and red onions, being mindful this is a sautéed dish and the pan needs to keep moving the whole four minute cooking process. Remove from heat; add herbs, salt and pepper and then it is ready to plate.

Place vegetables in the center, spoon potatoes on top, then chicken. Drizzle sauce atop the chicken then dollop sauce around the plate.

THE INFERNO BURGER

Ingredients

2 lbs certified Angus Beef (80/20 blend)

5 4-inch brioche bun

2 tsp cajun Seasoning

5 medium slice Pepper Jack Cheese

1 head iceberg lettuce, quartered

1 red onion, sliced

1 or 2 ripe tomatoes, sliced

10 oz pickled jalapenos

Sriracha Mayo:

1/4 cup liquid egg yolks

1 tsp fresh chopped garlic

Pinch kosher salt

2 cups canola oil

2 tbsp sriracha sauce

Tobacco Onions:

1 medium yellow onion, sliced thin

1 cup milk

2 cups cajun seasoned flour

2 cups canola oil for frying

Directions

Sriracha Mayo Procedure:

1. In food processor combine liquid egg yolks, fresh garlic and kosher salt.

2. Mix ingredients until smooth and slowly add the oil until mixture is thick and smooth.

3. Stir in Sriracha sauce and mix until incorporated.

(CONTINUED)

Burger Procedure:

1. *Heat grill to medium high heat for ten minutes.*

2. *Portion beef into 6 oz balls and then flatten and round to make burger patty. Be careful not to over mix as the beef will get tough. (A small dimple in the middle of the patty will keep the beef from balling up as it's cooked.)*

3. *Season both sides of patty generously with Cajun spice and place on hot grill. Cook for 5 to 6 minutes and then an additional 5 minutes.*

5. *While the burger is cooking thoroughly coat yellow onions in milk and then toss in Cajun flour making sure to coat all the onions with the flour.*

6. *Fry onions in hot oil until lightly browned and then remove to a paper towel lined plate.*

7. *Toast brioche bun on cooler part of grill until lightly browned.*

8. *Add pepper jack cheese to burger and let melt.*

9. *Add lettuce, tomato, onion, and jalapenos to bottom of the bun, place burger on bottom bun, and top with fried tobacco onions and sriracha mayo. Serve with salted fries and enjoy.*

PASTA PRIMAVERA

Ingredients

1 cup small broccoli florets

1 small zucchini, sliced

1 small red pepper, in strips

1 cup snow peas, trimmed

1/4 cup butter or margarine

1 cup cream, warmed

1 lb fresh pasta

Fresh grated imported parmesan

Fresh black pepper to taste

Directions

In a large skillet, sauté broccoli, zucchini, red pepper, and peas in butter until crisp-tender. Add cream and black pepper, cook briefly until slightly reduced. Serve over cooked pasta and sprinkle with parmesan. Serve immediately.

Jennifer Lawrence | Actress

CHICKEN POT PIE

Ingredients

1 cup each of chopped organic carrots, celery and onion

2 cups chicken broth

1 tsp salt

1 tsp pepper

4 cups organic cooked chicken breast

1 stick butter

1/2 cup flour

1 cup half and half

Pillsbury pie crust

Directions

Sauté butter for 10 minutes. Add flour, half and half and chicken broth to the mixture. Stir in veggie mix and add salt and pepper. Add in chicken breast. Put pie crust in greased casserole dish and pour mixture into casserole dish. Bake for 40 minutes at 400 degrees.

BLACK BEAN BURGERS

Ingredients

2 *16 oz cans of black beans drained and rinsed (or 3 cups drained cooked black beans)*

1 *jalapeño, deseeded*

1/2 *onion, chopped*

1 *small bunch of cilantro*

3 *eggs*

1 *tbsp chili powder*

2 *tbsp cumin powder*

1 1/2 *cups whole wheat breadcrumbs*

1/2 *tsp each, salt and pepper*

Parchment paper

Directions

In a food processor, combine half of the black beans, jalapeño, onion, cilantro and spices. Combine until smooth and the vegetables are finely chopped. Add the other half of black beans and pulse until quickly to blend the beans, but still leave some texture. Remove the black bean mixture and place in a large bowl. Add the eggs and breadcrumbs and combine with until smooth. Form into patties with clean hands, placing patties between layers of parchment paper. Recipe should yield 8-12 patties depending on the size. Freeze for 2 hours or longer to help the patties stay together on the grill. Extras can be frozen indefinitely and saved for future use.

To cook:
Lightly spray the patties with nonstick spray before placing on grill. Cook patties on a preheated grill, cooking about 6 minutes per side. Serve with all the fixins. I recommend Thai Chili sauce and sliced avocado on a bun.

Roger Burkman

CHICKEN FETTUCCINI NOODLES

Ingredients

Alfredo sauce "Savory Bacon" flavor

Fettuccini noodles

Thin sliced chicken breast strips

Roasted garlic virgin oil

Greek seasoning

Directions

Cut the chicken strips into thirds then add your Greek season. Heat frying pan to medium with roasted garlic virgin oil and chicken. Start boiling the fettuccini. Drain oil and natural juices from chicken and then add Alfredo sauce, heat on low. If you want you can pour the sauce over the fettuccini in a large container or serve separate.

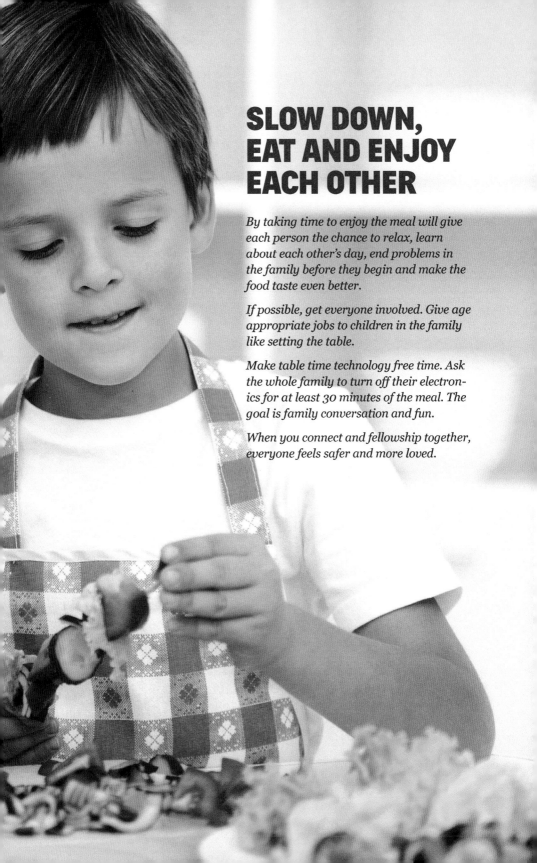

SLOW DOWN, EAT AND ENJOY EACH OTHER

By taking time to enjoy the meal will give each person the chance to relax, learn about each other's day, end problems in the family before they begin and make the food taste even better.

If possible, get everyone involved. Give age appropriate jobs to children in the family like setting the table.

Make table time technology free time. Ask the whole family to turn off their electronics for at least 30 minutes of the meal. The goal is family conversation and fun.

When you connect and fellowship together, everyone feels safer and more loved.

SHRIMP CASSEROLE

Ingredients

2 *cups cooked rice*

1 *can cream of mushroom soup*

3/4 *lb cooked shrimp*

1/2 *cup cubed cheddar cheese*

2 *tsp butter*

2 *tsp chopped green pepper*

2 *tbsp chopped onion*

1 *tbsp lemon juice*

½ *tsp Worcestershire sauce*

1/4 *tsp pepper*

Directions

Combine all ingredients; pour into greased casserole dish. Bake covered at 350 degrees for 30 minutes.

EDEN ISLE CHICKEN

Ingredients

4 *boneless, skinless chicken breast*

1 *cup sour cream*

1 *pkg cream cheese*

1 *can Cream of Chicken soup*

Directions

Wrap the chicken in bacon. Mix the sour cream, cream cheese and Cream of Chicken soup together. Spread cream mixture over chicken and bake covered for 2 hours at 325 degrees. Serve over egg noddles or wild rice.

Note: *You can choose to make this healthier by substituting low fat sour cream (or fat free) and low fat cream cheese (or fat free). It doesn't taste quite the same, but it's still good. To make it even healthier, you could always serve it over whole wheat pasta.*

"Here's a recipe from my mother. When I was a kid, this was my FAVORITE meal. It was my birthday tradition. Family dinners were an important part of my life growing up. We were all so busy during the day, and it was really the first time we'd all sit down together. Some of my most cherished moments revolve around sitting in the kitchen with my mom while she was making dinner. Hope this recipe is helpful!"

Colin Mayfield

CREAMY CAJUN CHICKEN PASTA

Ingredients

8 oz whole-wheat fusilli or rotini

1 tbsp canola oil

2 slices bacon, chopped

1 large sweet onion, halved and thinly sliced

1 lb boneless, skinless chicken breast, trimmed and cut into 1-inch pieces

1 medium green bell pepper, sliced

3 cloves garlic, minced

4 tsp Cajun seasoning (see Tip)

1/2 tsp freshly ground pepper

1 tbsp all-purpose flour

1 can (28 oz) crushed tomatoes

1/3 cup reduced-fat sour cream

1/2 cup sliced scallions for garnish

Directions

1. Bring a large pot of water to a boil. Cook pasta until just tender, 8 to 10 minutes or according to package directions, then drain.

2. Meanwhile, heat oil in a Dutch oven over medium heat. Add bacon, onion and cook, stirring occasionally, until beginning to brown. Add chicken, bell pepper, garlic, cajun seasoning and pepper. Cook stirring, until onion and bell pepper are beginning to soften, about four minutes.

3. Add flour and stir to coat. Add tomatoes and their juice; bring to a simmer. Cook, stirring often, until sauce is bubbling and thickened and chicken is cooked through. Remove from heat. Stir in sour cream.

4. Stir pasta into the sauce. Serve sprinkled with scallions, if desired.

Tip: We used a Cajun spice blend that contains salt. If you have a blend without salt (check the ingredients label), season the sauce with salt to taste.

MOM'S 3-CHEESE MAC & CHEESE

Ingredients

1/2 box of Barilla elbow macaroni

8 oz of Veleveeta cheese

8 oz sharp cheese

8 oz white cheddar cheese

1/2 stick of butter

1 cup of half & half

1 pinch of salt and black pepper

Sprinkle top with Panko bread crumbs

Directions

Sprinkle top with Panko bread crumbs and bake at 350 for 35-40 minutes.

FETTUCCINE WITH MUSHROOMS & PROSCIUTTO

Ingredients

3 tbsp olive oil

3 tbsp butter

1 lb fresh mushrooms, sliced

1/2 lb prosciutto, cut in bits

2 large tomatoes, peeled and chopped

1/4 tsp ground nutmeg

1 tsp sage leaves

1 cup heavy cream

1 lb fresh fettuccine or pasta of your choice

Salt

Fresh ground pepper

1 cup fresh grated parmesan

1/2 cup chopped italian parsley

Directions

Heat olive oil and butter in a large skillet, add mushrooms and cook until lightly browned (approximately 10 minutes). Add the prosciutto, tomatoes, nutmeg, sage and cream. Cook on high until sauce is somewhat thickened (4-5 minutes, be careful not to burn). Cook pasta al dente and drain, return to pot and add salt and pepper to taste. Add sauce and half the parmesan. Serve immediately with the remaining parmesan to sprinkle on top.

SPAGHETTI WITH CLAM SAUCE

Ingredients

1 *can (10 oz) baby clams*

1 *jar (6 oz) select oysters*

2 *oz butter*

1/4 *cup olive oil*

1/3 *cup chopped fresh italian parsley*

1 *lemon*

2 *garlic cloves, minced*

1 *lb fresh egg spaghetti*

Fresh ground pepper

Directions

In a small saucepan, sauté garlic in butter and olive oil. Chop oysters and add them with baby clams and juice. Peel and chop lemon rind, very fine. Add rind, parsley, and squeeze lemon juice in the saucepan. Simmer for about 10 minutes. Cook pasta al dente, drain and return to warm pan pasta was boiled in. Add clam sauce to pasta and serve immediately, season with pepper to taste.

CHINESE MEAT BALLS

Ingredients

2 lbs ground lean round or chuck

1/2 cup diced onions

1 cup sliced carrots (1/4 inch thick)

1 cup sliced celery (1/4 inch thick)

1 pkg frozen baby lima beans

2 cups consommé

4 tbsp cornstarch

2 tbsp soy sauce or more

1/4 cup of water

Salt to taste

Directions

Brown small meat balls in fat with onions. Add consommé and all vegetables. Cover and cook for 15 minutes. The charm of the dish is the crispness of the vegetables.

In a small bowl mix the cornstarch, soy sauce and water. Add to the main dish, stirring constantly and cook only until thickened and clear. Serve with rice. Serves 6.

FETTUCCINE ALFREDO

Ingredients

1 lb fresh egg fettuccine

1 cup whipping cream

1 stick butter

1 cup fresh parmesan

Fresh ground pepper

Directions

Melt butter in large sauté pan and add cream. Bring sauce to near boil, stirring. Add parmesan gradually. Add cooked fettuccine to sauté pan, blending thoroughly. Serve immediately with pepper and remaining parmesan.

PASTA SALAD OF MANY COLORS

Ingredients

1 lb pasta of choice

1 red bell pepper, diced

1 lb fresh baby spinach

1 can medium black olives

1 small jar green olives

1/2 cup Italian dressing of choice

1/2 lb mozzarella cheese, small cubes

Directions

Prepare pasta and cool. Add red bell pepper, baby spinach, olives and dressing (add more dressing if desired). Chill for at least four hours. Add the mozzarella cheese cubes when serving.

Note: Try adding other veggies like broccoli, cauliflower, cucumbers (seeded), other colorful peppers, etc.

BASIC MEAT LASAGNA

Ingredients

2 *lbs italian sausage, ground beef, veal, or a mixture of*

1 *cup parmesan, grated*

3/4 - 1 *lb ricotta cheese*

1 *lb shredded mozzarella (about 8-10 thick slices)*

10-12 *slices mild provolone*

4-6 *cups marinara or tomato sauce of your choice*

1/2 *lb mushrooms*

1 *green pepper*

1 *medium onion*

6-8 *fresh lasagna sheets (will not need par-boiling)*

Italian seasonings

9x13 pan

Directions

Brown meat with pepper, onion, mushrooms. Drain excess fat. Add sauce and seasoning to taste. Layer 1/3 of the meat sauce on bottom of pan, add parmesan, ricotta, provolone, and a layer of pasta. Continue with additional 2 layers of sauce, cheese and pasta. Finish with mozzarella on top. Bake in oven 60-90 minutes at 350, covered. Check for doneness and may remove top to let brown. Let lasagna stand for 5-10 minutes before cutting. Uncooked lasagna may be frozen for baking another time.

Fresh vegetables may be substituted for meat to make vegetarian (carrots, zucchini, broccoli, etc.).

CHICKEN RANCH TACOS

Ingredients

3 cups cooked chicken, cut up

1 packet of taco seasoning (chicken or beef)

1/2 cup Ranch dressing

Taco shells (hard or soft)

Lettuce

Tomatoes and other toppings of choice

Directions

1. Heat skillet over med-high heat. Add chicken and warm for a few min utes. Sprinkle on the dry taco seasoning. DO NOT add any water! Heat for 5-7 minutes until heated through and powder is stuck to the chicken.

2. Add 1/2 cup of ranch dressing, heat an additional two to three minutes to warm through.

3. Serve in taco shells with all the fixings... plus an extra squirt of Ranch!

GLUTEN FREE MEATBALLS

Ingredients

1 lb Barbour Farms, LLC ground beef

1 fresh Barbour Farms, LLC fresh eggs*

1/4 cup 1% milk*

1/4 cup grated Parmesan cheese

2 tbsp fresh basil or parsley, chopped

1 tbsp fresh garlic (1-2 cloves), chopped

1/2 tsp oregano

1 tsp minced onion

1 tsp sea salt

2 tsp extra virgin olive oil

Olive or Canola oil cooking spray

Optional: Sprinkle smoked paprika and crushed red pepper for added flavor

Directions

1. Mix all ingredients well.

2. Roll mix into 2 tbsp sized balls (makes approximately 17 meatballs).

3. Poke holes in a lightly sprayed disposable aluminum pan and place balls in pan on top of grill.

4. Cook until desired temperature*.

5. You may also place on a cookie cooling rack that sits on top of a baking sheet and bake at 350 degrees.

*Whisk eggs and milk along with dash of sea salt and pepper.

SMOKED SPINACH & ROMA TOMATOES

Ingredients

12-16 *fresh baby or regular spinach washed*

1 *tbsp fresh garlic, minced*

Dash of sea salt

Dash of black pepper

Dash of crushed red pepper

2 *tbsp rice wine vinegar*

1 *tbsp liquid Aminos by Bragg*

Olice or Canola oil cooking spray

4-6 *medium size Roma tomatoes*

Dash of sea salt

Dash of black pepper

Dash of garlic powder

Olive oil

Directions

1. *Cut tops of Roma tomatoes and then cut in elongated halves.*

2. *In a bowl, drizzle olive oil on tomatoes and then sprinkle sea salt, black pepper and garlic powder.*

3. *Toss to coat all tomatoes evenly.*

4. *Place tomatoes directly on top rack of grill and cook until skins begins to peel. (You may also put coals to side of grill and place tomatoes indirectly on cooler part so hot coals are not directly below tomatoes).*

5. *After tomatoes cool, remove skins and cut each tomato half.*

ROASTED GARLIC

Ingredients

4-6 medium garlic cloves, peeled
Olive or Canola oil cooking spray

Directions

1. Place peeled garlic cloves in aluminum packet sprayed with olive oil.

2. Place on grill and cook until garlic softens or starts to brown.

3. When garlic has cooled, use kitchen utility scissors to cut garlic into smaller pieces.

GLUTEN FREE PASTA

Ingredients

1 box of Barilla gluten free pasta of your choice
Olive oil
Sea salt

Directions

While meatballs, spinach and tomatoes are cooking, cook pasta al dente as directed on box. Add a touch of olive oil to water to prevent pasta from sticking. Add approximately 2 tbsp of sea salt to season pasta while cooking. When pasta is finished cooking, toss pasta in cold water to prevent further cooking. Spray pasta with olive oil cooking spray.

PUTTING IT ALL TOGETHER

Directions

1. In same pan you boiled pasta in, spray olive oil cooking spray to coat bottom and put on medium heat. Add cut roasted garlic, smoked Roma tomatoes and toss in smoked spinach.

2. Sauté over medium heat tossing all ingredients lightly. Add veggie broth and let it simmer (only a few seconds).

3. Then toss in pasta and sauté until sizzling and steamy. Remove from heat, plate and garnish with parmesan cheese and a basil sprig.

Erica Coghill | WLKY 32

VEGGIE BEAN WRAP

Ingredients

2 *wheat tortilla shells*

1 *cup black beans*

2/3 *cup of shredded cheese*

1 *cup baby kale (or your choice of greens)*

1/2 *tamato, diced*

1/2 *avocado, sliced*

1 *tbsp sour cream*

1 *tbsp hot sauce*

Directions

Warm black beans in microwave for one minute. Layer one tortilla shell with 1/2 cup of black beans and shredded cheese. Microwave for 20 seconds, then layer with baby kale, diced tomatoes and sliced tomatoes. Roll-up tortilla shell and top-off with sour cream and hot sauce. Makes 2 servings.

"I treasure every meal with my family. As much as a healthy meal provides nutrition, in my family it also provides a moment to connect. We talk about our days and share laughs over meals. However, we don't always share the same cravings and usually whip-up our own thing. I am a pescatarian (meaning the only meat I eat is fish & shellfish) and black beans are my "go-to" food. They are a great source of protein and are super tasty in this wrap."

SWISS STEAK

Ingredients

2 lbs round steak (cubed to 1") cube steak

3 tbsp flour (I use whole grain wheat flour)

2 tbsp olive oil

1 large onion

2 tbsp Worcestershire Sauce

1 can (3 oz) of tomato paste

4 cups water

Salt and pepper to taste

Directions

Coat steak in flour, salt & pepper, brown in skillet and set aside in a large dish or Dutch Oven along with the onion. Deglaze skillet with water, tomato paste and Worcestershire sauce. Pour the liquid over the steaks. Set oven to 300 degrees and bake for 2 1/2 hours. Serve with pasta, noodles or mashed potatoes.

Ben Pine | WHAS 11

CLASSIC CHICKEN DIVAN

Ingredients

2 bags (10 oz) of fresh or frozen broccoli spears

1/4 cup butter or margarine

6 tbs flour

2 cups chicken broth

1/3 cup whipping cream

3 tbs dry white wine

1/4 cup parmesan cheese

3 chicken breasts, cooked

1/2 tsp salt and pepper

Directions

Cook broccoli and place in an 8x8 (if doubling recipe 9x13) pan. Melt butter and blend in flour. Add salt and pepper. Whisk in chicken broth. Cook over medium high heat, stirring regularly until mixture thickens and bubbles. Stir in cream and wine. Pour 1/2 mixture over broccoli. Top with chicken. Add Parmesan cheese to rest of sauce and pour over chicken.

Bake at 350 for 20 minutes or until sauce bubbles. You can place under a broiler until sauce is golden if desired.

SAUCY MEATBALLS

Ingredients

1 lb pork

1 lb ground sirloin

1 lb ground chuck

1 small yellow onion

1 cup grated Parmesan cheese

1 tbsp basil

1 tbsp oregano

1 tbsp roasted red pepper

1 egg

Pinch of salt

Pinch of pepper

4 bottles (12 oz) Heinz Chili sauce

3/4 cup grape jelly

Directions

1. Preheat oven to 400 degrees.

2. Combine all ingredients except Heinz Chili Sauce and grape jelly in large mixing bowl.

3. Form small, golf ball size portions and lay on a baking sheet with at least a 1/4" rim to catch the grease. Cook 15-18 minutes.

4. Dump meatballs into crock pot. Pour Heinz Chili sauce over meatballs, and heat on low for one hour. Add grape jelly, heat another hour, then serve.

FAMOUS ITALIAN RECIPE

Ingredients

6 large chicken breasts, halved, deboned and skinned

1 clove garlic, crushed

2 medium onions, chopped

1 tbsp dried parsley

1/2 tsp thyme

1 tsp basil

1 tbsp cinnamon

5-6 mushrooms, sliced

2 cans tomato paste

1 pkg (24 oz) of spaghetti

1 cup parmesan cheese

Salt and pepper

Directions

In a large heavy pot, brown onions, garlic and parsley with non-stick cooking spray. Add tomato paste (2 cans of water to 1 can tomato paste), thyme, basil, cinnamon, mushrooms and salt & pepper (to taste). Stir until smooth. Add chicken, bring to a boil and simmer for one hour.

Remove chicken to heated serving dish and keep warm. Combine spaghetti and sauce, top with parmesan cheese and serve.

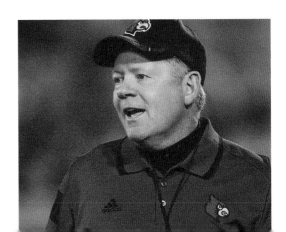

Derek Anderson | NBA and UK Star

CHICKEN, SWEET POTATOES & BROCCOLI

Ingredients

- **2** *free range boneless, skinless (if available) chicken breasts*
- **2** *tbsp coconut cooking oil*
- **1/2** *cup chicken broth*
- **2** *whole sweet potatoes*
- **2** *bundles of fresh broccoli*

Directions

1. *Pre-heat the oven at 375 degrees.*

2. *Put the coconut oil in a skillet/baking dish. Put chicken in the pan and place in the oven. After 15 minutes, turn chicken so it can brown on both sides. After a total of 30 minutes, pour in the broth and cook an additional 20-30 minutes.*

3. *While the chicken is cooking, clean the sweet potatoes. Place on ungreased cooking sheet and place in the oven. Cook approximately 35 minutes. Do not add anything to the sweet potatoes. They are naturally sweet and seasoned.*

4. *Place 3 to 4 cups of water in a sauce pan. Once water comes to a boil, place broccoli in the pan. To keep crisp cook for 10 minutes. If you prefer to cook longer do to your preference.*

VEGETARIAN PASTA ROSA

Ingredients

16 oz penne pasta

12 oz assoted chopped vegetables (such as broccoli, mushrooms, black and green olives, red peppers, fresh garlic and white onions)

4 oz heavy whipping cream

2 oz butter (unsalted)

2 oz grated Parmigiano Reggiano cheese (grated Parmesan calso works)

1/2 tbsp dried basil leaf

1/2 tbsp dried oregano

1/2 tsp granulated garlic

1 can (8 oz) tomatoes

1 tbsp extra virgin olive oil

1-2 oz chopped parsley

1-2 oz shredded Percorino Romano cheese

Sea salt to taste

Fresh ground pepper to taste

Flat, italian or french bread

Directions

1. Cook the Penne pasta in lightly salted boiling water for approximately 10 minutes or until done. Drain into a colander, rinse with cold water and set aside.

2. In a separate pot over low heat, mix heavy whipping cream, 2 oz of butter, grated parmigiano reggiano cheese, a half tbsp of dried basil leaf, add sea salt and freshly ground pepper to taste. Continuously stir over low heat and gradually raise the heat to dissolve cheese and thicken the sauce until it coats the back of the spoon. Remove from heat.

3. Place canned tomatoes (we use Italian San Marzanos) into a blender. Add a tbsp of extra virgin olive oil, garlic, basil leaf, dried oregano, 1/2 tbsp

(CONTINUED)

of sea salt. Purée in blender until thoroughly mixed. Pour into separate pot and cook over medium-high heat until the sauce begins to boil – stir so sauce does not stick or burn.

4. Cover bottom of a skillet with olive oil and add chopped vegetables over medium-high heat. Sauté vegetables approximately 2-3 minutes until they start to brown and onions become translucent. Lightly add salt and pepper.

5. Turn heat to medium and add Alfredo and Marinara Sauces to the skillet, mix sauces thoroughly with vegetables for approximately 1 minute.

6. Add Penne Pasta to skillet and continue to mix over medium heat for 2-3 minutes until noodles, vegetables and pasta are thoroughly combined and coated with sauce.

7. Divide across two full-sized plates. Serve with hot bread of your choice. Sprinkle grated Pecorino Romano cheese and chopped parsley on top.

THE HOT BROWN

Ingredients

2 oz whole butter

2 oz all purpose flour

8 oz heavy cream

8 oz whole milk

14 oz roasted turkey breast, sliced

2 slices Texas toast (crust trimmed)

4 slices crispy bacon

2 Roma tomatoes, sliced in half

1/2 cup Pecorino Romano cheese, plus 1 tbsp for garnish

Salt and pepper to taste

Paprika

Parsely

Directions

In a two-quart saucepan, melt butter and slowly whisk in flour until combined and forms a thick paste (roux). Continue to cook roux for 2 minutes over medium-low heat, stirring frequently. Whisk heavy cream and whole milk into the roux and cook over medium heat until the cream begins to simmer, about 2-3 minutes. Remove sauce from heat and slowly whisk in Pecorino Romano cheese until the Mornay sauce is smooth. Add salt and pepper to taste.

For each Hot Brown, place one slice of toast in an oven safe dish and cover with 7 oz of turkey. Take the two halves of Roma tomato and set them along side the base of turkey and toast. Next, pour one half of the Mornay sauce to completely cover the dish. Sprinkle with additional Pecorino Romano cheese. Place entire dish under a broiler until cheese begins to brown and bubble. Remove from broiler, cross two pieces of crispy bacon on top, sprinkle with paprika and parsley, and serve immediately.

The Brown Hotel "Hot Brown"

Eric Flack | WAVE 3 NEWS

COUSCOUS

Ingredients

2 boxes (8 oz) pearled couscous

1/2 cup Craisins

1/2 or cup lima beans

1/4 or 1/2 cup crumbled feta

1/4 cup sliced almonds

Directions

Prepare couscous as directed on box. Add remaing ingredients and mix together. I usually eyeball all ingredients, as much or as little as you like.

MAMA MAYFIELD'S SHRIMP ALFREDO

Ingredients

1 *lb of shrimp*
1 *cup of celery cut horizontally*
1 *cup of red onion cut in strips*
1 *cup of broccoli florets*
1/2 *of a pound box of spaghetti*
1 *jar of Alfredo sauce*

Directions

Boil spaghetti noodles and set aside. Sauté onions, broccoli and celery in butter or olive oil. Add shrimp and Alfredo sauce. Add in pasta.

CHICKEN DELIGHT

Ingredients

Chicken Delight
1/2 *cups bulk mayonnaise*
1/2 *bag of egg noodles (boil as directed)*
4-6 *slices of Velveeta*

Directions

Pour Cream of Chicken over cooked egg noodles. Layer with the slices of Velveeta. Bake at 350 for 30 minutes. Serves 4-6.

Julee Rosso & Sheila Lukins (Matt Lauer's favorite, NBC Today)

CHICKEN MARBELLA

Ingredients

4 chickens, 2 1/2 lbs each, quartered
1 head of garlic, peeled and finely pureed
1/4 cup dried oregano
1/2 cup red wine vinegar
1/2 cup olive oil
1 cup pitted prunes
1/2 pitted Spanish green olives
1/2 capers with a bit of juice
6 bay leaves
1 cup brown sugar
1 cup white wine
1/4 italian parsley or fresh coriander (cilantro), finely chopped
Course salt and freshly ground black pepper to taste

Directions

1. *In a large bowl combine chicken quarters, garlic, oregano, pepper and coarse salt to taste, vinegar, olive oil, prunes, olives, capers and juice, and bay leaves. Cover and let marinate, refrigerated, overnight.*

2. *Preheat oven to 350 degrees.*

3. *Arrange chicken in a single layer in one or two large, shallow baking pans and spoon marinade over it evenly. Sprinkle chicken pieces with brown sugar and pour white wine around them.*

4. *Bake for 50 minutes to one hour, basting frequently with pan juices. Chicken is done when thigh pieces, pricked with a fork at their thickest, yield clear yellow (rather than pink) juice.*

5. *Transfer chicken, prunes, olives and capers to a serving platter using a slotted spoon. Moisten with a few spoonfuls of pan juices and sprinkle with parsley or cilantro. Pass remaining juices in a sauceboat.*

EATING ON A BUDGET

It takes a bit of planning to save money and make a budget work. Plan meals and even snacks for your family according to an established budget. Here are a few tips to help:

1. *Check for sales and coupons in the local paper or on-line.*

2. *Use your loyalty card.*

3. *Do not go grocery shopping when you are hungry or when you don't have time. An empty belly and a full schedule will cost you. Take your time when you shop.*

4. *Make a list and stick to it.*

5. *Buy store brands if cheaper.*

6. *Compare unit prices listed on shelves to get the best price.*

7. *Check prices on bulk or family sizes... they usually cost less.*

8. *Fresh fruits and vegetables in season cost less.*

9. *Stay away from pre-cut fruits and vegetables, individual cups of yogurt, and instant rice and hot cereal. They may be more convenient but they are usual more expensive.*

10. *Don't forget to incorporate leftovers to make a full meal.*

CHICKEN & SAUSAGE JAMBALAYA

Ingredients

6 *turkey bacon slices, chopped*

1 1/2 *cups celery, sliced*

1 *cup uncooked brown rice, uncooked*

1 *cup onion, chopped*

1 *cup green pepper, chopped*

1 *can (14 1/2 oz) tomatoes*

1/2 *lb cooked smoked turkey sausage, cut in 1/2" pieces*

1 1/2 *cups water*

1/2 *cup barbeque sauce*

1 *tsp salt*

1/4 *tsp cayenne peppers*

1 1/2 *cups cooked chicken, diced*

Directions

Fry bacon until crisp in a large, deep skillet. Stir in celery, rice, onion and green pepper. Cook while stirring for 5 minutes. Add undrained tomatoes, sausage, water, barbecue sauce, salt and cayenne. Stir, bring to a boil. Cover and simmer for 20 minutes, stirring occasionally. Add chicken. Serves 4.

PIZZA CASSEROLE

Ingredients

1 lb ground beef
1/3 cup chopped onion
1/2 diced green bell peppers
1 can (4 oz) mushrooms
1/2 tsp salt
8 oz spaghetti, cooked
2 cans (10 oz) of pizza sauce
2 cups shredded mozzarella cheese

Directions

Preheat oven to 350 degrees. Grease 9x13 pan. Brown the beef with the onion and green pepper in a a skillet, drain the grease. Stir in mushrooms, salt, cooked spaghetti and spoon into baking dish. Pour sauce on top and sprinkle with a layer of cheese. Bake until casserole is bubbling, about 30 minutes.

FLORIDA ORANGE RICE

Ingredients

1 cups white rice
2 tbsp sugar
1 1/2 oranges, cut into pieces
1 cup dream whip

Directions

Combine cooked rice, sugar, oranges and dream whip. Stir and chill for one hour before serving.

MEATLOAF

Ingredients

2 lbs ground chuck

5 slices white bread

2 large eggs, slightly beaten

1 cup crushed saltine crackers

1 can (6 oz) tomato paste

1/2 cup celery, finely chopped

1/2 cup onion, finely chopped

3 tbsp Worcestershire sauce

1/4 cup Dijon mustard

2 tbsp fresh parsley, chopped (more for garnish)

1 1/4 tsp salt

1 1/4 tsp ground black pepper

2 tbsp brown sugar, firmly packed

1 tbs fresh lemon juice

Directions

Preheat oven to 350 degrees. Line a rimmed baking sheet with aluminum foil. Spray the foil with nonstick cooking spray.

In a large bowl, combine the chuck, crackers, celery, onions, Worcestershire sauce, 2 tbsp of Dijon mustard, parsley, 1 tsp of salt and pepper, the eggs, half the can of tomato paste, and mix together.

Arrange white bread on the bottom of a baking sheet and place the beef mixture on top. Shape the mixture into a 12-inch loaf.

Combine the brown sugar and lemon juice with the remaining tomato paste, Dijon mustard, salt and pepper. Spread mixture over the meatloaf and tent with foil. Bake until meat thermometer registers 165 degrees (about 50 minutes). Remove foil during last 10 minutes of cooking. Let meatloaf stand for 10 minutes before slicing. Garnish with fresh parsley if desired. Serves 6-8.

Connie Leonard | WAVE 3 NEWS

CHILI CORN CONNIE

Ingredients

1-1 1/2 *lbs ground beef*

1 *medium to large onion, chopped*

1 *bag or can of corn*

1 *can chili ready tomatoes*

1 *can tomatoes with diced chilies*

1 *pkg chili seasoning*

1 *tsp cumin*

Salt and pepper

Sour cream

Shredded cheddar cheese

Directions

Brown ground beef and onion, drain. Mix in seasoning and cumin with tomatoes and corn. Serve with cheese and sour cream.

DAVID VOGEL'S MEAT LOAF

Ingredients

1-1 1/2 lb ground beef (1/4 of this may be pork)

1 egg yolk

2 tbsp chopped parsley

1 tbsp soft butter

1 tbsp bread crumbs

1 tsp lemon juice

1 tsp salt

1/4 tsp pepper

1/2 tsp onion juice

Directions

Pre-heat oven to 350 degrees. Combine above and shape into loaf. Place the loaf in a lightly greased pan. Bake for one hour.

Baste at intervals with: 1/4 cup butter, 1/4 cup vegetable stock or 1/4 cup boiling water plus 1/2 pkg of dried soup mix. Pour remainder over top.

CHEESY CHICKEN & RICE

Ingredients

1 *box of yellow rice*

1 *can cream of chicken*

1 *can whole kernel corn*

1 *small onion*

3-4 *chicken breasts*

1/2 *pkg (16 oz) shredded cheddar cheese*

Directions

1. Place chicken breasts in the bottom of slow cooker. Chop up onion and toss on top of the chicken. Spoon cream of chicken soup over the chicken and onions.

2. Cover slow cooker and let it cook on low 7-8 hours or high for 3-4 hours.

3. Prepare rice according to package directions.

4. When chicken is done cooking, shred the chicken and then drain and add the corn, cooked rice and cheddar cheese into the chicken mixture.

5. Stir all together and let it heat together for 10 minutes or so.

SPICY EGGPLANT PASTA

Ingredients

- **2** medium eggplants
- **3** tbsp olive oil, divided
- **1** medium onion, chopped
- **2** cloves garlic, minced
- **2** cups plum tomatoes, chopped or 14 oz can crushed tomatoes
- **1** tbsp fresh oregano, or 1 1/2 tsp dry oregano
- **2** red pepper flakes, plus extra for finishing
- **1/4** cup fresh basil, chopped, plus extra for finishing
- **1** lb linguine pasta

Directions

1. Cut the eggplants crosswise into 1-inch thick slices. Lay slices on a baking sheet, salt well on both sides, and set aside for half an hour or so.

2. Preheat the oven to 425 degrees.

3. Drizzle two tablespoons of olive oil over the eggplant, tossing the slices to coat them. Sprinkle with sea salt and black pepper. Arrange them in a single layer on the baking sheets and roast them until they're tender and browning, about 20 minutes.

4. While the eggplant roasts, heat remaining tbsp of olive oil on low heat in a large saucepan. Add onions and minced garlic, and sauté until onions are soft. Add tomatoes, oregano, pepper flakes, and basil. Continue to cook, stirring occasionally, till sauce has thickened (approximately 10-12 minutes). When the eggplant is ready, remove from oven, chop into 1-inch pieces, and add it to the sauce. Continue to simmer on very low heat.

5. Bring a large pot of salted water to boil. Add pasta and cook until al dente, about 8 minutes. Drain pasta and gently fold in the sauce. Top pasta with additional chopped basil and red pepper flakes to taste.

TURKEY MEATLOAF

Ingredients

3 cups chopped yellow onions (2 large onions)

2 tbsp good olive oil

2 tsp kosher salt

1 tsp freshly ground black pepper

1/3 tsp fresh thyme leaves (1/2 teaspoon dried)

1 cup Worcestershire sauce

3/4 cup chicken stock

1 1/2 tsp tomato paste

5 lbs turkey breast

1 1/2 cups plain dry bread crumbs

3 extra large eggs, beaten

3/4 cup ketchup

Directions

1. Preheat oven to 325 degrees.

2. In a medium sauté pan, over medium-low heat, cook the onions, olive oil, salt, pepper, and thyme until translucent, but not browned, approximately 15 minutes. Add the Worcestershire sauce, chicken stock, tomato paste and mix well. Allow to cool to room temperature.

3. Combine the ground turkey, bread crumbs, eggs, and onion mixture in a large bowl. Mix well and shape into a rectangular loaf on an ungreased sheet pan. Spread the ketchup evenly on top. Bake for 1 1/2 hours until the internal temperature is 160 degrees and the meatloaf is cooked through (a pan of hot water in the oven under the meatloaf will keep top from cracking). Serve hot, at room temperature, or cold in a sandwich.

MEATS

POULTRY

SEAFOOD

Illustration by Chase

Lonnie Ali

QUICK AND EASY PULLED BBQ CHICKEN

Ingredients

1 *medium vidalia or sweet onion, peeled and sliced thin*

1 *rotisserie chicken, skinned, and deboned*

1 *large bottle of sweet honey BBQ sauce*

Directions

Place onion slices on the bottom of slow cooker or ceramic crock pot. Take deboned chicken and pull into shreds. Place chicken into crock pot on top of onion slices. Pour BBQ sauce over chicken and spread evenly. Place top on crock pot and turn heating dial on low or set timer to 2-4 hours. During cooking period, remove top and mix bbq sauce thoroughly through chicken. Once heated, serve on soft whole wheat hamburger buns. Complete meal with sides of coleslaw, fresh corn or green salad.

Note: *If you don't have a crock pot, place ingredients into a heavy oven proof pan with a tight fighting lid. Place in oven at 300 degrees for 2-3 hours.*

JACK FRY'S

PORK SHOULDER

Ingredients

1 medium pork butt, about 6-8 pounds

1 cup olive oil

1 tbsp cumin

1 tbsp coriander

1 tbsp paprika

1 tbsp granulated garlic

1 tbsp onion powder

1 orange, juice and zest

2 quarts chicken stock

2 quarts water

Directions

Rub shoulder well with olive oil, spice mixture, orange zest and juice, salt and pepper. If possible, let marinate in refrigerator overnight but not necessary. Place roast in oven at 375 until skin becomes dark brown. Transfer to a roasting pan with seasoned chicken stock and water (should come up to about half of the roast). Cover with foil and braise for up to 12 hours at 275 or until fork tender. Remove skin, fat, bone and gently pull meat apart, making sure not to shred too much. Re-warm pulled meat in chicken stock or your favorite barbecue sauce.

JACK FRY'S

HERB & LEMON ROASTED POTATOES & SQUASH

Ingredients

3 lbs fingerling potatoes

2 zucchini

2 squash

1 bunch fresh sage, minced

1 bunch fresh Italian parsley, minced

4 cloves of garlic, minced

2 lemons, zested

1/2 cup olive oil

Directions

Slice fingerling potatoes in half lengthwise and cut zucchini and squash into half-moons. Toss the potatoes in olive oil and season with salt and pepper. Roast at 350 until a knife passes through them without resistance. While the potatoes are cooking heat a large pan on medium-high heat. Add olive oil and zucchini and squash and sauté until starting to brown. Add minced garlic, herbs and lemon zest right before the squash is tender, set aside. When the potatoes are done cooking combine them and the squash mixture into a large mixing bowl. Squeeze lemon juice and a little fresh olive oil over everything and toss until mixed evenly. Serve immediately.

Baptist Health/Milestone
wellness
center

AVOCADO STUFFED CHICKEN BREASTS

Ingredients

4 chicken breasts, pounded flat

2 ripe, fresh California avocados peeled, seeded and sliced

3 tbsp lime juice

1 tsp lemon pepper

1 tsp garlic powder

1/2 fresh, minced basil leaves

1 large tomato, seeded and diced

1/2 cup sweet onion, chopped

2 tbsp cracked peppercorns (optional)

1/4 tsp cayenne pepper

Directions

Place the chicken breasts on a flat, working surface. Mix all the remaining ingredients together, except for the peppercorns. Reserve half of the mixture and divide onto the chicken breasts. Roll up the breasts, tucking in ends and place in a lightly oiled baking dish. Sprinkle with the peppercorns. Bake in a preheated oven at 350 for 45 minutes, or until chicken is fork tender. After removing from oven, cut each breast in half. Place on a platter with the reserved avocado mixture. Garnish platter with fresh basil, lime slices, small tomatoes and avocado slices (or any of these in different combinations).

CRAB CAKE MIX

Ingredients

1 lb jumbo lump crab meat

1 Panko bread crumbs

1 lb claw crab meat

1 3/4 tsp lemon juice, fresh

2 whole eggs

3/4 tsp white pepper

1 3/4 tsp kosher salt

1/2 oz scallions, minced

2 tbsp italian parsley, minced

3/4 tsp Tabasco

1/2 tbsp Wocestershire

1/2 tbsp Gulden's Spicy Mustard

1/2 cup mayonnaise

Directions

1. In a large stainless bowl whisk together ingredients except crab meat and bread crumbs until well incorporated.

2. In a large stainless bowl gently combine claw crab meat and bread crumbs with wet mixture. Mix by hand until well incorporated.

3. Very carefully fold in jumbo lump; be careful to not break up the crab meat. Store in refrigeration until ready to portion.

SALMON FILET WITH SUN DRIED TOMATO TOPPING

Ingredients

4 *salmon filets with skin on (6 oz portions)*

3/4 *cup sun dried tomatoes, finely chopped*

2 *tbsp unsaledt butter, softened*

2 *tbs grapeseed oil*

1 *tbsp Mrs. Dash original blend seasoning*

Directions

1. *Remove salmon filets from refrigerator and allow to come to room temperature.*

2. *Make topping: In a small bowl, combine sun dried tomatoes and butter. Mix thoroughly and set aside.*

3. *Preheat grill or cast iron griddle to medium heat. Brush filets with grape seed oil and season with Mrs. Dash seasoning.*

4. *Generously spray cooking surface with cooking spray. Place filets on the grill, skin side up. Grill side without skin for approximately 2-3 minutes, watching carefully not to burn.*

5. *Flip to skin-down side and grill for 3-4 minutes. Cover with foil until skin is crispy.*

6. *Preheat oven to 375 degrees. Place generous portion of sun dried tomato topping on top of filets. Heat for another 6-7 minutes, until sun dried tomatoes begin to crisp. Serve immediately.*

Katherine Kington | WAVE 3 NEWS

FISH IN FOIL

Ingredients

2 lbs frozen fish steaks

1/2 cup chopped onion

1/2 cup chopped green pepper

2 tbsp butter

1/2 cup ketchup (maybe plan on a cup)

1/2 tsp garlic salt

1 bay leaf

Salt and pepper

Directions

Rip off four (4) foil pieces that could hold a fish and some sauce wrapped up. Cook onion and green pepper in butter. Add seasonings and ketchup and simmer 10-15 minutes. Place Fish in foil. Pour ¼ of sauce over each fish. Fold tightly. Place foil packages in shallow baking dish. Bake 15-20 minutes at 500 degrees. Serves 4.

"Family Dinners are just as important to me now as they were when my brother and I couldn't reach the table. In fact, more so. The same round wooden table may have a new coat of paint, and be a darker shade, but the scratches in its surface tell the tales of us growing up. We had family dinners every night. Family dinners were a nightly ritual. It wasn't until I was older I realized that not everyone sat around the table at dinner. I remember one friend saying, "it's so boring! why would we do that? We go out or watch tv". But when do you talk? These days we have 100 things to do, most of us wearing three hats or more before the sun sets. You're running around, trying to stay organized in a chaotic life, but when you sit down at the dinner table the world slows down for a little bit."

Chelsea Rabideau | WHAS 11

EASY PARMESAN CRUSTED TILAPIA

Ingredients

3/4 *cup grated parmesan cheese*

2 *teaspoons paprika*

1 *tablespoon dried parsley*

4 *tilapia filets*

Olive oil

Directions

Turn oven to broil (high setting).

In a dish combine the cheese, paprika, and parsley. Add salt and pepper to taste. Coat the filets in olive oil and dredge in the cheese mixture.

Place on a baking sheet and put under broiler for about 10 minutes.

Kelsey Starks | WHAS 11

CROCKPOT PORK

Ingredients

3 *lb pork loin roast (approximate weight)*

1 *jar banana peppers (mild or spicy)*

1 *envelope onion soup mix*

Directions

Put in crockpot in the morning on slow and it will be ready when you get home after work! Serve on buns with dill pickles and onions.

CHICKEN FRIED STEAK

Ingredients

Chicken breasts, skinless and boneless

2 cups skim milk

1 egg

2 1/2 cups flour

1/4 cup bread crumbs

2 tsp black pepper

2 tsp garlic powder

2 tsp Mrs. Dash Table Blend

2 tsp Mrs. Dash Caribbean Blend

2 tsp Old Bay Blackened Seasoning

Directions

Start with skinless boneless chicken breast. Cut them in half (vertical) which will leave them about a quarter of an inch in thickness. Use a meat tenderizer (mallet) to beat out the breast meat to make it ultra thin.

In a medium size bowl add milk, egg, pepper, Mrs. Dash seasoning. Stir vigorously. Place chicken in the mixture and allow to marinate for 10 minutes.

Take chicken breast from mixture and put them in the bag with flour and spices. Make sure they are thoroughly coated.

Use a large skillet for frying. Fill the skillet about 1/4 inch deep with olive or canola oil. Make sure the oil is very hot. Place coated chicken breast into skillet. Cook approximately 6-8 minutes on each side (temperature and time may vary depending on your stove). Flip your chicken to the other side as you notice golden brown edges around the ends of your breast. Allow your chicken to cook approximately the same time on each side.

Remove the golden brown chicken breast for the skillet and allow them to drain flat on a plate covered with paper towels.

John Boel | WAVE 3 NEWS

BEER BATTERED WALLEYE

Ingredients

12 oz flour
12 oz beer
Walleye
Oil for deep fryer

Directions

Clean Walleye and filet into narrow strips. Mix beer and flour (make sure there are no lumps). When deep fryer oil is hot, coat Walleye strips with batter and drop them in fryer. Remove from fryer when golden brown and place on cookie sheet with paper towel to soak up draining fryer oil.

PARMESAN CHICKEN

Ingredients

1 1/2 lbs split, boneless, skinless chicken breasts (or strips)
1 envelope (1 oz) Italian dressing mix
1/2 Parmesan cheese
Cooking spray

Directions

1. Preheat over to 350 degrees and spray a baking sheet with cooking spray.

2. Rinse chicken breasts and pat dry.

3. In a pie plate, mix Italian dressing mix and Parmesan cheese.

4. Spray chicken breasts with cooking spray and dip into dressing mixture to coat both sides. Place chicken on on the prepared baking sheet. Spray top of chicken with cooking spray.

5. Bake 30 minutes. If extra browning and crispness is desired, broil for 5 minutes.

Katherine Kington | WAVE 3 NEWS

LEMON CHICKEN BREASTS

Ingredients

4 chicken breasts, boneless with skin on

1/4 Good Extra Virgin Olive Oil

3 tbsp minced garlic

1/3 cup dry white wine (optional)

1 tbsp grated lemon zest (2 lemons)

2 tbsp freshly squeesed lemon juice

1 1/2 tsp dried oregano

1 tsp fresh thyme leaves

Kosher salt and black pepper

1 lemon

Directions

1. Preheat oven to 400 degrees.

2. Warm olive oil in a small saucepan over medium-low heat, add garlic and cook for one minute, don't let burn. Turn off heat, add white wine, lemon zest, lemon juice, oregano, thyme, and one teaspoon of salt and pour into a 9x12 baking dish.

3. Pat chicken breasts dry and place them skin side up over the sauce. Brush chicken with olive oil and sprinkle them liberally with salt and pepper. Cut the lemon in eight wedges and tuck it among the pieces of chicken.

4. Bake for 30 to 40 minutes, depending on size of the chicken breasts, until the chicken is done and the skin is lightly browned. If the chicken isn't browned enough, put it under the broiler for two minutes. Cover the pan tightly with aluminum foil and allow to rest for 10 minutes. Sprinkle with salt and serve hot with the pan juices.

COOKIES

CAKES

CONFECTIONS

Illustrations by Saymee (top) and Ethan (bottom)

AUNTIE'S FRUIT DELIGHT

Ingredients

3 *egg whites*
1 *cup granulated sugar*
1/4 *tsp cream of tartar*
1 *cup soda crackers*
1 *tsp vanilla*
1 *envelope Dream Whip*
Fruit Pie Filling or Fresh Fruit

Directions

Beat egg whites until frothy but not stiff. Add sugar and cream of tartar and beat until peaks form. Stir in crackers and vanilla. Put in greased 8x8 pan. Bake at 350 for 20 minutes, then let cool. Prepare Dream Whip according to directions and cover cool cake. Top with fruit pie filling of fresh fruit.

Note: *Can double for 13x9x2 pan.*

BLUEBERRY PIZZA

Ingredients

1 1/2 *cups plain flour*

1 *cup chopped pecans*

1 *tbsp sugar*

2 *dashes of salt*

1 1/2 *sticks melted margarine*

Filling:

1 *pkg (8 oz) cream cheese (room temperature)*

2 *cups powdered sugar*

1 *container (8 oz) Cool Whip*

1 *can blueberry pie filling*

Directions

Crust: *Mix all ingredients well. Press into a 13-inch pizza pan. Bake at 350 degrees for 10-15 minutes or until light brown. Cool completely.*

Filling: *Cream sugar and cream cheese. Fold in Cool Whip and spread on crust. Spread pie filling on top and refrigerate.*

*"**How to enjoy:** After a night of dancing to the Louisville Crashers, go home and retrieve your fruit pizza from the fridge, fix a glass of cold milk, chocolate milk, or decaf coffee and enjoy... then, get some sleep, wake up and enjoy for breakfast too..."*

– Mark Maxwell (lead singer, the Louisville Crashers)

CHOCOLATE CHIP COOKIES

Ingredients

1 3/4 cup plain flour

1 1/4 tsp baking soda

1 1/4 tsp baking powder

1 1/2 tsp maldon sea salt

1 1/4 cup unsalted butter

1 cup packed brown sugar

3/4 cup demerara sugar

2 eggs

2 tsp vanilla extract

2 1/2 cups bitter chocolate chips/chunks

Directions

1. Sift dry ingredients together. Cream the butter and sugar. Add eggs one at a time and the vanilla. Add dry ingredients to the butter-sugar mix ture, then chocolate chips. Mix until just combined.

2. The cookie dough should be cool and firm, so wrap and chill. The dough gets better and better and ideally should be chilled overnight.

3. Preheat oven to 375. When dough has had time to chill roll into 2 oz balls and flatten ever so slightly. Place on baking paper. Sprinkle each cookie with a little maldon sea salt.

4. Bake for 10 minutes. A little less, a little more, depending on your oven – until they are golden brown but still soft. Leave to cool on wire rack.

EASY CAKE RECIPE

Ingredients

1 *pkg (16 ounce) angel food cake mix*

1 *can (20 ounce) crushed pineapple with juice*

1 *container (12 ounce) frozen whipped topping, thawed (optional)*

Directions

1. *Preheat oven to 350 degrees. Spray a 9x13 inch pan with vegetable oil spray.*

2. *In a large bowl, combine cake mix and pineapple (with juice). Mix until well blended.*

3. *Pour batter into prepared 9x13 inch pan. Bake at 350 for 25 minutes or until golden brown. Let cool. Serve with whipped topping if desired.*

SNOW ICE CREAM

Ingredients

1 *gallon of fresh snow*

1 *cup of white sugar*

1 *tbsp of vanilla extract*

2 *cups of milk*

Directions

Collect about a gallon of fresh snow. Stir in sugar and vanilla to taste, then stir in just enough milk for the desired consistency. Serve at once.

SWEET POTATO PIE

Ingredients

6 *sweet potatoes, cooked and peeled*

1 1/2 *cups of sugar*

3 *eggs*

2 *tbsp vanilla extract*

1 *tsp cinnamon*

1/4 *tsp allspice*

1/4 *tsp nutmeg*

1 *can evaporated/condensed milk*

2 *tbsp of self rising flour*

1 *pie crust*

Directions

Combine all ingredients and bake at 375 degrees for 20-25 minutes.

OREO TRUFFLES

Ingredients

36 *Oreo cookies, finely crushed, divided*

1 *pkg (8 oz) Philadelphia Cream Cheese, softened*

4 *pkg (4 oz) Baker's Semi Sweet*
Chocolate broken into pieces, melted

Directions

Reserve 1/4 cup cookie crumbs. Mix cream cheese and remaining cookie crumbs until blended. Shape into 48-1" balls. Dip in melted chocolate and place on wax paper-covered rimmed backing sheet. Sprinkle with reserved cookie crumbs. Refrigerate for one hour or until firm.

Coach Mo | Biggest Loser Contestant

APPLE TREAT

Ingredients

1 large (3 1/4") Golden Delicious apple

1 tsp ground cinnamon

2 tsp Truvia (or other natural sweetner)

Directions

Preheat oven to 375 degrees. Core the apple 3/4 of the way through, leaving a 1/2" seal at the bottom. Trim skin around the top of the apple and place in an ungreased baking dish. Combine cinnamon and sweetener and pour most of the mixture into the center of the apple; sprinkle the rest on top of the apple and in the bottom of the baking dish. Pour water 1/4" deep in the baking dish. Bake uncovered for 30 to 40 minutes, until apple is tender. Spoon the mixture in the baking dish over the apple while it is baking.

FROZEN BERRY-NUT PARFAIT

Ingredients

1 cup fat-free Greek style yogurt

1/2 cup fresh blueberries

1/3 cup diced frozen strawberries

1-2 packets of Truvia (or other natural sweetner)

2 tsp vanilla extract

1/4 cup walnuts, toasted and chopped

Directions

In a food processor, combine yogurt, blueberries, strawberries, sweetener, vanilla and process until smooth. Stir in nuts. Transfer mixture to a pint container, cover, and freeze for about 30 minutes, or until just frozen, then serve.

GRANDMOTHER MARY'S LEMON PIE

Ingredients

Lemon zest of about half lemon rind

Juice of three (3) lemons

1 can Eagle Brand Sweetened Condensed Milk

3 extra large egg yolks

1 graham cracker crumb pie crust (homemade or store bought)

Directions

Whip yolks until frothy. Add milk, juice and lemon. Place in pie shell and bake for 20-25 minutes in a 350 degree pre-heated oven.

"This is very similar to a Key Lime Pie. My daddy's all-time favorite (which he kindly told me this past father's day after I've made him approximately 45 different key lime pies. Really?!) Please forgive the lack of measurements. My grandmother's recipes were all in her head. This is the only one on paper which I cherish."

Famous Tea

LEMONADE POPPY SEED POUND CAKE

Ingredients

1 box lemon cake mix

1 box lemon instant pudding mix

2 tbsp poppy seeds

1/4 cup vegetable oil

4 eggs

1 cup Milo's All Natural Lemonade

Glaze:

1/3 cup sugar

1/2 cup Milo's All Natural Lemonade

1/2 tsp lemon extract

Powdered sugar

Directions

Cake:

Combine ingredients and beat until mixed well. Don't over beat. Fold into a greased and floured tube/Bundt pan. Bake at 350° F for 40 minutes or until a toothpick inserted in center comes out clean and center of cake springs back to touch. Let cake stand 10 minutes. Turn onto a cake plate.

Glaze:

In small saucepan on cook top, combine sugar, Milo's All Natural Lemonade & lemon extract. Bring to a rolling boil. Pour over warm cake. Let sit 30 minutes. Sift powdered sugar over the top, if desired.

MILE HIGH APPLE STACK PIE

Ingredients

Crust:

6 cups self-rising flour

1/2 tsp baking soda

1 cup (2 sticks) butter, plus extra for pans

4 eggs, beaten

1/2 cup molasses

1 cup sugar

1 tsp vanilla extract

1 tsp ground cinnamon

2/3 cup milk

Flour for the work surface

Filling:

1 lb firm tart apples, peeled, cored, and sliced

Sugar

Ground cinnamon

Ground allspice

Powdered sugar, for topping

Directions

Preheat oven to 300. Prepare six 9-inch round cake pans with butter.

Sift together the flour and baking soda into a medium bowl. Cut in the butter with a fork and mix until the mixture forms coarse crumbs. In a large bowl, beat together the eggs, molasses, sugar, vanilla, cinnamon, and milk. Gradually add flour mixture to egg mixture, stirring well after each addition. The dough will resemble bread dough. Turn the dough onto a floured board or cloth and knead for 1 minute. Divide dough into 6 equal parts and roll each out into a 9-inch circle. Place them into cake pans and bake until golden, 10 to 15 minutes. Transfer the pans to racks and let cool.

(CONTINUED)

Meanwhile, put the apples in a pot with two cups of water, cover and cook over low heat until apples are tender but not mushy, about 20 minutes. Strain and discard the extra liquid. Return the pulp to the pot, measuring it one cup at a time. For each cup of pulp, add 1/2 cup sugar, 1/4 tsp cinnamon, and 1/8 tsp allspice. Cook over low heat until sugar is dissolved and mixture is thick.

Remove the cake layers from the pans and spoon the filling between the layers, stacking one on top of the other and ending with a cake layer on top. Sprinkle with powdered sugar. Cover with a cake cover or plastic wrap. Let the cake sit at room temperature for one or two days before serving.

BLUEGRASS COOKIES

Ingredients

2 3/5 *cup all purpose flour*

1 *tsp baking soda*

3/4 *tsp baking powder*

1/2 *tsp salt*

1 1/8 *cup butter*

1 *cup pitted prunes*

3/4 *cup raw sugar*

1 *cup brown sugar*

2 *eggs*

2 *tsp almond extract*

1 3/5 *cup hemp seed*

6 *oz sliced almonds*

6 *oz white chocolate chips*

Directions

1. *Preheat oven to 325 degrees.*

2. *Sift together dry ingredients (flour, baking soda, baking powder, salt) and set aside.*

3. *In separate bowl cream butter with raw and brown sugars.*

4. *Add eggs, one at a time, while continuing to beat, then almond extract.*

5. *Slowly add dry mixture, pausing 3 times to scrape down the sides and bottom of mixing bowl, till well incorporated.*

6. *Stir in hemp seed, sliced almonds, and white chocolate chips.*

7. *Scoop cookies onto baking sheet and flatten each a bit with your hand.*

8. *Bake at 325 degrees for 8-12 minutes (ovens vary), till cookies are golden brown on edges.*

BANANA SPLIT ICE CREAM PIE

Ingredients

1 chocolate cookie pie crust (9-inch) or 20 chocolate wafer sandwich cookies

2 firm, medium-sized bananas, sliced

1 qt Blue Bell Strawberry Ice Cream, softened

1 can (20 oz) crushed pineapple, drained

1 cup whipping cream

1 cup pitted prunes

1/4 cup chopped walnuts or almonds

Maraschino cherries

Directions

To make crust if using cookies: Mix cookie crumbs with ¼ cup melted butter or margarine. Press into a 9-inch pie plate. Arrange bananas over bottom of crust. Spread ice cream in an even layer over bananas. Top with drained pineapple. Spread whipped cream over all and sprinkle with nuts. Place pie in freezer for 4 hours or until firm. Garnish with cherries, if desired. Makes one 9-inch pie.

CAROLYN'S COCONUT CUPCAKES

Ingredients

1 1/2 cups organic whole wheat pastry flour

1 tsp baking powder

1 tsp baking soda

1/2 tsp sea salt

1/4 cup organic coconut flakes

1/3 cup melted coconut oil

3/4 cup organic maple syrup

1 cup organic coconut milk

2 tsp organic vanilla extract

1 tsp vinegar (white wine or apple cider is good)

Frosting:

28 oz unsweetened organic coconut milk

1/2 cup agar flakes

Pinch of salt

2 tsp vanilla

1/2 cup organic maple syrup

Directions

1. Preheat oven to 350 degrees. Place cupcake liners in pan.

2. In a medium sized bowl, sift and mix flour, baking powder, baking soda and coconut flakes. In a separate smaller bowl, combine and whisk together oil, maple syrup, vanilla, vinegar and salt.

3. Pour wet mixture into dry mixture and gently fold them together with a rubber spatula until smooth.

4. Fill cupcake liners about 1/2 to 3/4 full and place in oven for 20 minutes. If not done, check every 5-10 minutes until there is no batter on the tooth pick. Let cool before icing.

(CONTINUED)

Frosting:

1. *In a medium saucepan, combine and mix coconut milk and agar flakes. Let sit for at least 10 minutes. Add salt, vanilla and maple syrup.*

2. *Over medium-high heat, bring coconut mixture to a boil, whisking often and scraping the agar from the sides and bottom of pot with a rubber spatula.*

3. *Reduce heat to very low and cook partially covered, stirring and scraping often until agar is dissolved (about 15-20 minutes).*

4. *Pour the coconut mixture into a shallow pan and chill until set.*

5. *In a food processor, combine the coconut mixture with cashew butter. Process until smooth and silky.*

BANANA SPLIT TERRINE

Ingredients

1/2 *gallon Blue Bell Dutch Chocolate Ice Cream*

2 *pints Blue Bell Strawberry Ice Cream*

1 *pint Blue Bell Homemade Vanilla Ice Cream*

1 *banana, chopped*

3 *tbsp chopped maraschino cherries*

2 *tbsp chopped crystallized ginger*

1 *jar (5 oz) jar pecan topping with syrup*

Directions

Line a 9x5x3-inch loafpan with heavy-duty plastic wrap, smoothing wrinkles as much as possible. Spread Blue Bell Dutch Chocolate on bottom and up sides of pan, and freeze until firm. Spread Blue Bell Strawberry ice cream on top and up sides of chocolate ice cream, and freeze until firm. Combine Blue Bell Homemade Vanilla and next three ingredients; spread over strawberry ice cream, and freeze until firm. Remove terrine from pan; peel off plastic wrap. Cut terrine into 6 wedges. Drizzle with pecan topping, and garnish, if desired. Garnish with maraschino cherries with stems. Makes 6 servings.

CARAMEL-TOFFE BOMBE

Ingredients

1 1/3 *cups gingersnap cookie crumbs (about 20 cookies)*
1/4 *cup butter or margarine*
1 *pint Blue Bell Homemade Vanilla Ice Cream, softened*
4 *English toffee-flavored candy bars (1.4 oz), crushed*
Praline sauce

Praline Sauce:

1/2 *cup firmly packed brown sugar*
1/2 *cup half-and-half*
1/4 *cup butter or margarine*
1/4 *cup slivered almonds, toasted and chopped*
1 *tsp vanilla extract*

Directions

Line a 2-quart bowl with heavy-duty plastic wrap. Set aside. Combine cookie crumbs and butter; press mixture into prepared bowl. Combine ice cream and crushed candy, and spoon into bowl. Cover and freeze at least 8 hours. To serve, let bowl stand at room temperature 5 minutes; invert onto a serving plate. Carefully remove bowl and plastic wrap. Cut into wedges, and serve immediately with warm Praline Sauce. Makes 10 to 12 servings.

Praline Sauce:

Combine first 3 ingredients in a small saucepan; bring mixture to a boil over medium heat, stirring occasionally. Boil 2 minutes, stirring occasionally. Remove from heat; stir in almonds and vanilla.

Sherlene Shanklin | VIPP Communications

BANANA PUDDING

Ingredients

2 *ripe bananas*

5 *large egg yolks*

2 *cups of 2 percent and/or whole milk*

1/2 *cup sugar*

2 *tsp vanilla extract*

1 *tsp banana flavoring*

2 *tbsp butter (unsalted if available)*

1/2 *pkg (12 oz) vanilla wafers and/or graham crackers*

1 *container (8 oz) frozen whipped topping, thawed*

Pinch of salt

Directions

In a large bowl, whisk eggs, corn starch, cold milk sugar, salt, vanilla, butter and banana flavoring until smooth. Put milk in a saucepan and bring it to a boil. Combine both mixtures. Cook until mixture is thick, approximately two minutes. Once mixture is cool. Put in the refrigerator for up to four hours.

Take pudding out of refrigerator and begin to layer the dessert. Line the bottom of a 9-inch dish with vanilla wafers/crackers. Arrange sliced bananas evenly over wafers crackers. Spread with pudding mixture. Continue until you have a couple of layers. Make the top layers whipped topping. With the cookies leftover crumbling and sprinkle over the top of the dessert and then put back into the refrigerator to chill. Serves 6 people.

BOURBON DARK CHOCOLATE TRUFFLE

Ingredients

1/2 lb dark chocolate

1/4 cup bourbon

1/4 cup heavy cream (room temperature)

1/2 lb dipping chocolate or tempered chocolate

Directions

For the Ganache:

Slowly melt chocolate in a double boiler, stirring constantly. When chocolate is completely melted and slightly above body temperature or 110 degrees, set aside.

Combine heavy cream and bourbon, then stream into chocolate while constantly stirring.

When the chocolate and cream have fully combined, forming the ganache, pour into a shallow container and place it into the refrigerator.

For Dipping the Truffles:

When the ganache has set up and is firm enough to scoop, begin using a #4 scoop, producing balls about 1" in diameter. Hand roll them to maintain perfectly round ganache balls. If they begin to melt in your hands, place them back into the refrigerator for 10-12 min and try periodically washing your hands in cold water while hand rolling to keep the heat from your hands down. Do not place ganache balls back into refrigerator after all balls have been formed.

Prepare your dipping chocolate (per package instruction) or tempered chocolate, following tempering methods.

Allow ganache balls to come fully to room temperature and begin using a dipping fork to dip ganache balls into chocolate. After dipping truffles, place them onto wax paper or parchment.

OREO DESSERT

Ingredients

1 *package Oreo cookies*

1/2 *cup butter*

1 *pkg (8 oz) cream cheese*

1 *container (12 oz) Cool Whip*

1 *cup powdered sugar*

2 *pkgs of vanilla pudding*

3 *cups 2% milk*

Directions

1. *Crush Oreos and mix together with melted butter (1st layer).*

2. *Beat cream cheese, 1 cup cool whip and powdered sugar (2nd layer).*

3. *Mix milk and instant pudding (3rd layer).*

4. *Top with whipped cream (4th layer).*

Dawne Gee | WAVE 3 NEWS

PEACHES & CREAM DESSERT

Ingredients

3/4 cup all purpose flour

1 pkg (4 serving) vanilla instant pudding

3 tbsp margarine melted

1/2 cup sugar

1 tbsp sugar

1 tsp baking powder

1 beaten egg

1/2 cup milk

1 can (16 oz) sliced peaches

1 pkg (8 oz) cream cheese, softened

1/2 tsp ground cinnamon

Directions

In a bowl mix flour, pudding mix and baking powder. Combine egg, milk and margarine. Add to dry ingredients. Mix well and spread into greased 8x8x2 inch baking dish. Drain peaches but reserve 1/3 cup of the peach juice. Chop peaches into small pieces and sprinkle atop batter. Beat together cream cheese, the ½ cup of sugar and the reserved peach juice. Pour atop peaches in pan over batter.Combine one tbsp of sugar and cinnamon, sprinkle over all. Bake at 350 degrees for 45 mins and cool.

FRUIT SALSA & CINNAMON CHIPS

Ingredients

2 *kiwis, peeled and diced*

2 *Golden Delicious apples, peeled, cored and diced*

8 *oz raspberries*

1 *carton (16 oz) of strawberries, diced*

2 *tbsp white sugar*

1 *tbsp brown sugar*

3 *tbsp any fruit flavor preserves*

Cinnamon chips (various brands in stores)

Directions

1. *In a large bowl, thoroughly mix kiwis, apples, raspberries, strawberries, white sugar, brown sugar and fruit preserves. Cover and chill in the refrigerator at least 15 minutes.*

2. *Serve chilled fruit mixture with Cinnamon Chips. Salsa can also be served with cinnamon graham crackers or cinnamon pita chips.*

Note: *Best when made and eaten the same day.*

FRUIT PIZZA

Ingredients

Pie crust:

2 cups of finely chopped pecans

2 cups of flour

1 1/2 stick melted butter

1/2 cup of sugar

Fruit whip spread:

1 regular size container of cool whip

1 regular size cream cheese

1 bag of powdered sugar

Directions

1. Mix all ingredients together for the crust. Mix well and pat into a large size pan until dough is flat and as thin as you would like but not too thin. Let cook util nice and brown.

2. Mix fruit whip slow and well and spread over the cooled pecan crust.

3. After pecan crust is cool and fruit whip has been spread on top. Place your favorite pie filling on top (strawberry, cherry, blueberry... we've never used apple, but why not?). Then pile on every fresh fruit known to man. Every fruit you can find that is in season. Slice and eat !!!!!

Jean West | Medical Digest

EASY CAKE MIX COOKIES

Ingredients

Any cake mix
1/2 cup of vegetable oil
2 whole eggs

Directions

Preheat oven to 350 degrees. Mix all ingredients together in a large bowl. Drop by spoonful on a cookie sheet and bake for 8-10 minutes. Add chocolate chips for extra treat.

Bob Kay | Legendary WAVE 3 Broadcaster

BOB KAY'S DUMP CAKE

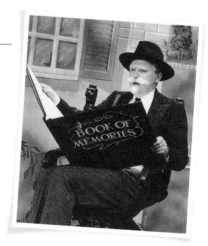

Ingredients

1 large can crushed pineapple
1 can cherry pie filling
1 pkg yellow cake mix
1/2-1 cup chopped nuts
1 cup (2 sticks) oleo

Directions

Grease 9x13 pan. Dump in the undrained crush pineapple and spread to fill corners. Dump in cherry pie filling and even it around. Dump in dry cake mix and sprinkle it to cover evenly. Scatter nuts over cake mix. Cut oleo into pats and place on top. DON'T MIX!!!! Bake in preheated 350 degree oven for one hour until nicely brown.

WHITE CHOCOLATE CREME BRULEE FONDUE

Ingredients

2 oz white chocolate wafers

2 oz white chocolate mixture

1 oz (4 pumps) Monin Créme Caramel Syrup

1/2 oz carmelized sugar

8 sprays Cookal Caramel Alcohol Spray

Directions

Add dry wafers to fondue pot. Add white chocolate mixture on top of wafers. Add Créme Caramel Syrup to the chocolate. Stir mixture five times with a long-handed teaspoon. Serves 2.

BOURBON CREME BRULEE FONDUE

Ingredients

4 oz white chocolate wafers

1 oz (4 pumps) Monin Créme Caramel Syrup

1/2 oz Bourbon Vanilla Sugar shards

1/4 Buffalo Trace

Directions

Add dry wafers to fondue pot. Add Créme Caramel Syrup to the chocolate. Add the Bourbon Vanilla Sugar shards and Buffalo Trace. Stir mixture five times with a long-handed teaspoon. Serves two.

Janelle MacDonald | WAVE 3 NEWS

RASPBERRY ROYAL CHEESECAKE

Ingredients

1 cup butter or margarine

1 1/4 cup graham cracker crumbs

1 pkg (12 oz) cream cheese, softened

3/4 cup sugar

2 eggs

1 tsp vanilla

1 container (8 oz) sour cream

3 tsp sugar

1/2 tsp vanilla

Red Raspberry Sauce:

1 pkg (10 oz) frozen red raspberries

3 tsp sugar

1 tsp cornstarch

1 tsp lemon juice

Directions

1. Preheat oven to 325 degrees.

2. Melt butter. Combine with graham cracker crumbs in small bowl. Mix well. Press crumb mixture into bottom and up the sides of 8-inch round glass baking dish.

3. Cream together cream cheese and 3/4 cup sugar. Add eggs one at a time. Blend in one tsp of vanilla. Pour mixture into crust.

4. Bake in 325 degree oven for 25 minutes, or until the center is almost set. Remove from oven and let stand five minutes. Increase oven temperature to 450 degrees.

5. Meanwhile, combine sour cream, three tbsp sugar and vanilla in bowl and mix well. Spread over cheesecake and bake in 450 degree oven for five minutes. Cool on a rack and then refrigerate for at least three hours.

BEVERAGES
SANDWICHES

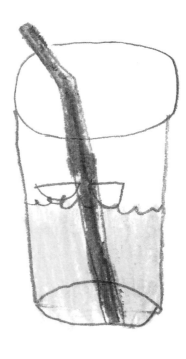

Illustration by Garret (left) and Chase (right)

CUBANO SANDWICH

Ingredients

2 *lb pork butt roast (bone removed)*
1/4 *or 1/2 cup Badia Complete Seasoning*
2-3 *cups Goya Mojo Marinade*

For Sandwiches:
Cuban or french bread
Boiled ham, thin sliced
Swiss cheese, thin sliced
Sliced pickles
Mustard
Pork from above

Directions

Cut/pull pork into chunks, place in roasting pan. Sprinkle with Badia Seasoning and then cover with Mojo. Cover with foil and roast at 350 degrees for 1 1/2 - 2 hours or until fork-tender. Makes 8 sandwiches.

Cut bread into 6-inch pieces and slice for sandwich. Place bread on hot grill and press with grill press or brick covered in foil. Stack ham, pickle and swiss, let melt on grill. Heat ¼ lb of Pork on grill. When bread is toasted, add mustard, pork and grilled ham/pickle/swiss combo. Press for 1 minute.

Dawne Gee | WAVE 3 NEWS

LEMON FIZZ

Directions

Squeeze one lemon for each glass

Put the lemon juice into the glass

Add 1 tablespoon or more of sugar

Add crushed ice to each glass

Fill with soda water

For fun you can add a drop of food coloring into your fizzy treat

"Better than a Kentucky State Fair Lemon Shake-up!"

STRAWBERRY YOGURT SMOOTHIE

Ingredients

1 1/2 cup fat free milk

1 container (8 oz) low fat vanilla yogurt

1 cup fresh or frozen strawberries

Directions

Place all ingredients in a blender and cover. Blend on high-speed until smooth. Serve immediately. Makes three 1 cup servings.

MILO'S.
Famous Tea

SWEET TEA OR LEMONADE GRANITA SLUSH

Ingredients

3 cups Milo's Sweet tea or Milo's Lemonade

Directions

Pour Milo's Sweet Tea or Milo's Lemonade into an 8x8-inch glass or ceramic baking dish. Cover and freeze until partially frozen (about one hour). Scrape with a fork, crushing any lumps. Freeze again, scraping with a fork every 30 minutes for one hour or until frozen. Scape into a glass and enjoy with a spoon. Makes 4 to 6 servings.

Terry Meiners | 84WHAS

GRILL CHEESE SANDWICH

Directions

Take two slices of bread, spray on butter, place in skillet, add favorite cheese, flip sandwich as cheese begins melting, let sizzle for another 20 seconds.

"VOILA! Best grilled cheese ever!"

EGGNOG

Ingredients

1/2 gallon whole milk

3 eggs, beaten

3/4 cup sugar

1/3 cup instant nonfat dry milk

1 packet (2 1/4 tsp) of gelatin

1/2 tsp cinnamon

1/2 tsp nutmeg

1/2 tsp rum flavoring

1/2 tsp vanilla flavoring

Directions

1. Stir together beaten eggs, the liquid flavorings, and 1 quart (4 cups) of the milk.

2. Blend Instant Nonfat Dry Milk, sugar, spices, and gelatin by stirring together thoroughly with a spoon in a small container.

3. Mix these dry ingredients into the milk mixture with a wire whisk.

4. Add the remaining milk.

5. Heat mixture to greater than 165 degrees in a microwave oven or double boiler and hold at that temperature for at least 30 seconds. Stir with a wire whisk a few times during and after heating.

6. Cool immediately in refrigerator. Stir before serving.

EGGNOG (LOW CALORIE)

Ingredients

1/2 gallon 2% or skim milk

1 egg, beaten

16 (1 gm packets) Acesulfame-K type sweetener

1/3 cup instant nonfat dry milk

3 tsp gelatin

1/2 tsp cinnamon

1/2 tsp nutmeg

1/2 tsp rum flavoring

1/2 tsp vanilla flavoring

Directions

Use the preparation procedure given for the original version substituting a
low calorie sweetener for the sugar. Other options are to use 1% fat or .5% fat
milks, rather than 2% fat or skim. All are available on the commercial market.
A table of the ranges of calories, fat, and cholesterol in the various formula-
tions appears below. A specific sugar substitute is listed in the ingredients for
the low calorie eggnog because sweetness equivalency to sugar varies widely
and sugar substitutes cannot be interchanged in recipes without making ad-
justments. If you prefer another sugar substitute or cannot obtain this one
you may recalculate the amount needed to obtain sweetness equivalent to 3/4
cup sugar as specified in the original recipe. Follow package equivalency
labels and directions as some sweeteners recommend replacing only a portion
of the sugar in a recipe.